Powerful Ideas in Teaching

Creating Environments Where Students Want to Learn

Mickey Kolis and Emily Bright Krusack

ROWMAN & LITTLEFIELD EDUCATION
A division of
ROWMAN & LITTLEFIELD PUBLISHERS, INC.
Lanham • New York • Toronto • Plymouth, UK

Published by Rowman & Littlefield Education
A division of Rowman & Littlefield Publishers, Inc.
A wholly owned subsidiary of The Rowman & Littlefield Publishing Group, Inc.
4501 Forbes Boulevard, Suite 200, Lanham, Maryland 20706
www.rowman.com

10 Thornbury Road, Plymouth PL6 7PP, United Kingdom

British Library Cataloguing in Publication Information Available

Library of Congress Cataloging-in-Publication Data

Kolis, Mickey, 1954-
Powerful ideas in teaching : creating environments where students want to learn / Mickey Kolis and
Emily Bright Krusack.
p. cm.
Includes bibliographical references.
ISBN 978-1-4758-0196-5 (pbk.) -- ISBN 978-1-4758-0197-2 (electronic)
1. Teaching. I. Krusack, Emily Bright, 1982- II. Title.
LB1025.3.K665 2012
371.102--dc23
2012034796

♾™ The paper used in this publication meets the minimum requirements of American
National Standard for Information Sciences Permanence of Paper for Printed Library
Materials, ANSI/NISO Z39.48-1992.

Printed in the United States of America

Contents

Acknowledgments

I am grateful to all the fantastic teachers who have shared lesson plans, brainstormed strategies, and listened after both the good and the bad classes. I'm a better teacher because of the community around me. My thanks to the Center for Excellence in Teaching and Learning at the University of Wisconsin–Eau Claire for starting our research group on learning. Mickey, your enthusiasm and your vision are contagious; it's been a pleasure to write this book with you. And—always—thank you to Matthew and my family for your support.

—Emily

I have had the pleasure of working with practicing classroom teachers for over twenty-five years: Sterling High School, Montana State University-Northern, and the University of Wisconsin–Eau Claire. The working knowledge classroom teachers compile is what good teaching is all about. Thanks to all of you for sharing your insights and strategies with me—and now with many other teachers.

I would also like to thank all my students for bearing with me as I learned the craft of teaching. I must admit that as I look back on my first years, I am embarrassed by what I thought good teachers knew and were like. Fortunately I have learned and changed over time.

I would also like to thank Emily for being such a wonderful colleague (and writer). She is professional in every sense of the word and collaborating with her for this book was a joy!

Finally, many, many thanks to my wife and family who keep me grounded and positive—no small task!

—Mickey

Foreword

"When you love your work that much—and many teachers do—the only way to get out of trouble is to go deeper in. We must enter, not evade, the tangles of teaching so we can understand them better and negotiate them with more grace, not only to guard our own spirits but also to serve our students well."[1]

What can we learn as we travel life's journey and become teachers? In the current educational climate, we face constant challenges and criticism regarding education in the United States. Critical comments by policy makers and corporate executives may blame the teaching profession, but they do not aim criticism at individual teachers. In poll after poll, the public affirms connections to local teachers and confidence in their performance. In addition, many of us can recount the story of a teacher or several teachers who not only had a profound influence upon what we learned but also inspired the best in us as learners for the rest of our lives.

This inspiration now seems to be peripheral; policy makers are uninterested in the lives and stories of individual teachers who are successful. Instead, collectively, teachers face intensely increased scrutiny and accountability. Systems are looking more closely at extensive national standards and holding teachers accountable for those standards in increasingly high-stakes assessment. The knowledge-based systems of the past have given way to new demands for students, requiring students to continue to access knowledge, understand the ways to process new ideas, and prepare to use knowledge in ever-changing situations. Yet the variability of student achievement remains amid unequal opportunities to learn and perform.[2]

Other countries have changed their place in the educational arena, realizing that the investment in human potential was critical. These countries, such as Singapore, Finland, and South Korea, have invested in the development of individual teachers with stunning success. These teachers are able to work with students, regardless of their backgrounds, and ensure success. How do they do it? Many of Kolis and Krusack's lessons provide keys to success related to teaching understandings that extend beyond content measured on achievement tests.

Every year, enthusiastic, committed teachers return to the classroom resolved to create a successful year for their students. Teaching is both professionally isolated and socially intense with students; there is little time for teachers to work with each other. Teaching is also complex. The development of a teacher's knowledge and skills occurs throughout a lifetime, often unchallenged and unappreciated except by the students in the classroom. Refining teaching requires ongoing attention to many aspects of practice. It includes the ongoing development of deep content knowledge, knowledge of pedagogy, and assessment.

But there is so much more to the social aspects of teaching. In refining, reflecting, and revisiting the ways in which a classroom is designed, teachers' relationships with their students are critical. Kolis and Krusack remind us, in inspirational yet very specific ways, the extent to which relationships tie to accountability. They poignantly describe the ways in which a teacher must listen to students and come to know their beliefs, challenges, and aspirations. They sharply return teachers' attention to an unemphasized conversation in today's highly charged debates. They provide "wisdom of practice" related to the teacher's journey toward engagement of students to produce a positive impact on student learning. They remind all of us who teach of our obligation to stop and consider the value-laden choices we make.

Teaching requires intense knowledge of how children learn and how they relate to and perceive the teacher in the classroom.[3] From whom do we learn? How do we make learning irresistible? Kolis and Krusack remind us that a deep understanding of and commitment to working with students enhances every opportunity to learn. They underlie the importance of teaching from a point of view that accounts for children's interests, optimizes opportunities for connections to their lives, and celebrates their creativity.

Investing in one's own teaching means taking risks and admitting that we can do better. For those willing to continue their professional teaching, Kolis and Krusack remind us that refining teaching is our life's work—and that the opportunity to share the joy of teaching reprioritizes and solidifies one's personal and professional commitment to teaching.

Kathe Rasch
Dean and Professor Emerita
Maryville University

NOTES

1. Palmer, Parker J. *The Courage to Teach: Exploring the Inner Landscape of a Teacher's Life*. Hoboken, NJ: John Wiley & Sons, 1998.

2. Darling-Hammond, Linda. *The Flat World and Education: How America's Commitment to Equity Will Determine Our Future*. New York: Teachers College Press, 2010.

3. Hammerness, K. et al. "How Teachers Learn and Develop," in *Preparing Teachers for a Changing World: What Teachers Should Learn and Be Able to Do*, ed. by Linda Darling-Hammond, John Bransford, Karen Hammerness, and Helen Duffy. San Francisco: Jossey-Bass, 2005, 358–389.

Introduction

Anyone who thinks teaching is easy hasn't spent much time in a classroom. There is so much to think about: teaching standards, content standards, student learning data, special education students, gifted students, English learner (EL) students, students of diversity—all in one classroom. It's enough to make your head spin.

The finer and finer slicing and labeling of our students makes teaching appear more and more complex. (Certainly the paperwork can be so!) Teaching *is* complex, and yet at its core it remains an interpersonal activity. We teach people, always have and always will. If we are lucky, we will also help them learn some content.

Many years ago I used to teach a graduate class for educators, and one activity that students had to do was called "pearls of wisdom." They were to imagine that they had just retired after thirty years as a classroom teacher and that they had been invited to give a talk to beginning teachers about their "pearls of wisdom." They had to list some ideas, then pick their top three "pearls" that had helped them become a successful teacher.

In their presentations, the teachers each had to tell a story to make their point. The class voted on the top three ideas. Over years of doing this exercise, I found that some ideas emerged every single time, no matter the audience, the grade level, or the location.

Powerful ideas in teaching exist at every level PK–16, in every content area. How they look and how they are implemented and modified depends upon the teachers themselves and their context.

This book is intended to help teachers focus on ideas that are deep and powerful—ideas that cut across all the finer slicing of student labels and lead to systemic change. In each chapter, you'll find key ideas that start broad and grow in complexity, inviting you to reflect on how you think about teaching and student learning. We'll delve into approaches to discipline, risk, and failure, to teaching with changing technology and making the most of assessment.

These are practical, hands-on issues that come up daily in the classroom. Because of the scope of this book, you won't find too many specific lesson plans or proscriptive "when x happens, do y." Teaching is interpersonal, which means there are always a complex series of factors at stake determining how you handle each situation. While this book won't preach exactly what to do, it will arm you with how to understand the situation within the larger context of long-term learning.

Feel free to read these chapters in any order you choose. Jump in where an idea appeals to you, double back—each chapter is designed to stand by itself. The ideas here are interconnected, and they will build upon each other no matter their order. It is, after all, your classroom, and you know best where you want to go next. As we'll talk about throughout the book, the most powerful learning happens when the learner is in control.

The other key idea you'll find running through this book is that you teach who you are. Your interests, your personality, your learning styles, and your experiences influence how you approach a classroom—and that's a good thing. Because you are at the center of how you teach, who you are matters.

Therefore, you'll find some of these topics to be as applicable personally as professionally. Reflection on our work inside the classroom is hard to separate from ourselves outside of the classroom. Teaching starts with the self. It cannot, and should not, have to be separated from what you think and care about, from how you treat others or the expectations you hold. Your vision for the modern education system, whether it's on the personal or systemic level, is part of how you teach. All these personal aspects are part of what drives you and makes your unique classroom work.

Each of these ideas is a pearl. The value is there. But what really makes it beautiful is when you pick it up, polish it, and display it for others to see. There is no one right answer. There are deep answers that seem to work across the board, but the personalization task is up to you.

You the reader have a choice—to make any of these ideas your own, or not. They depend upon you owning these thoughts—within your own context and dependent upon who you are as an individual and your learning. There are no simple answers. Knowledge is personal and earned; it cannot be given.

Ultimately, all learning is change. Deep learning involves owning and being responsible for that change. How precisely that looks will be different for every person who picks up this book.

Finally, a confession: most of these ideas are not new. They have been gathered over years of hands-on teaching and reading learning theorists. We simply haven't seen them in print one place before. That is one of the challenges of education: when teachers retire, too frequently their stores of knowledge leaves with them. This book is an attempt to keep that knowledge alive for the next generation of teachers.

What you do with it is up to you. That, we think, is part of the fun.

Chapter One

Mirror, Mirror on the Wall

There is a video called the "Selective Attention Test," readily available on YouTube, that does a wonderful job of getting students to reflect on how they think.[1] In the video, students wearing either white or black T-shirts bounce a basketball back and forth, and the task for onlookers is to count the number of times the students in white T-shirts pass the ball.

The students are moving as they bounce the ball, so you have to focus hard to make sure you don't miss a pass. If all you notice are the students in white T-shirts passing a ball, though, you fail the test. What you miss is a person in a gorilla costume walking calmly through the center of the throng, pounding its chest, and walking out.

Once you know it's there, it's hard to imagine how anyone could miss it. You can't get much more obvious than a gorilla. Yet every year in class, when asked who spotted the gorilla, only about half the onlookers raise their hands. Even those who claimed to see it the first time have a much larger reaction when we watch it again.

It's an amusing exercise for early in the school year, with an important point: sometimes, even when we're watching closely, we can still miss necessary information. Caught up with our busy teaching loads (and homework loads, for students), it's easy to see only what we want to see and hear only what we expect to hear. Learning from our experiences requires reflection—and that means stepping outside ourselves, viewing the world around us as observers rather than participants.

Just looking isn't enough. We have to learn how to reflect.

We are creatures of habit, and that means we hold to patterns—of thought, belief, and actions. We do what we do, believe what we believe, and think what we think because it appears to work for us.

A mirror reflects a reality, but how we interpret that reality is up to us. If we think someone is irresponsible, then no matter what they do, their actions are filtered through our lens of "irresponsibility." Students we peg as gifted or troublesome at the start of the year continue to strike us that way long after their behavior has changed.

The more we know how we learn, the more we recognize where our own preferences and blind spots fall. That recognition makes us stronger teachers in classes filled with a wide variety of needs.

There are other realities, of course, other perspectives that we have not considered, other points of view that explain the same set of phenomena in other ways. We are unconsciously unaware that our beliefs, actions, and thoughts are limiting our views of reality. In some ways, our individual lenses protect us, keeping us from being too overloaded with information to act. At other times, we keep to our way of seeing the world as a result of personal choice.

In either case, we have a tendency to stay comfortable with what we currently know, do, and believe. And that tends to make us dig in our heels and defend our point of view when presented with new experiences or new perspectives.

We dismiss alternative points of view without asking questions such as: What if the other point of view is correct? What experiences would I have had to come to that specific belief? Why do I believe what I believe? What experiences have I had that support my views? These kinds of questions ask us to examine our innermost selves so that we can make an informed decision rather than be held hostage by our current views.

> *Story: I grew up in a traditional nuclear family. My dad worked outside the home, my mom worked at home (even how I phrased that sentence is a function of learning—we used to say Mom "stayed" at home, not "worked" at home). When I got married, my wife and I both worked, and yet our first year of marriage was marred by my thinking that the husband came home and read the paper until dinner was served. I was a function of my past experiences.*
>
> *Until my wife made me aware of another reality, a different kind of "husband," I was limited by my own "thinking" (or lack thereof). Fortunately for our marriage, I was able to learn and change.*

Our ability to reflect upon our innermost selves is a measure of our ability to learn. Self-reflection clarifies where you are right this moment, your viewpoints, your knowledge (and knowledge gaps), your skill sets, and how you feel about change and growth. The more we take stock in where we currently are, the more aware we may become of where we need or want to go. Reflection is a powerful teaching tool, yes. It's also fundamental to personal growth.

WAYS OF REFLECTING

Learning theorist Donald Schön[2] broke down reflection into two different forms, based on when and why we are reflecting. He named them reflection-in-action and reflection-on-action, and both are worth a moment of exploration here.

Reflection-in-action has to do with the now. It's that in-the-moment, standing-in-front-of-the-class consideration that allows you to step back mentally and ask, "What's going on here?" It's the running analysis that happens when we read student body language and respond by asking a less complicated question or shifting gears. It's the consideration that we've just asked three analysis questions in a row and need to move on to something more complex. It's metacognition in action.

In a classroom setting, where we are always on the go, the first and easiest forms of reflection that we turn to are action-oriented. We think of reflection-in-action as a way to improve specific skills, including classroom management, assessment strategies, variety-of-instruction strategies, wait time, respondses to partially correct answers, and so on. By focusing on one or two specific skills at a time and responding to student feedback on the spot, we keep ourselves learning and the classroom running smoothly.

Reflection-on-action, on the other hand, is the thinking that happens before or after lessons when we have more time to focus. Stepping back after a lesson, for example, reflection-on-action allows us to say, "I thought they would respond this way to that activity, and instead they did this and that. I thought this lesson would move more quickly—or more slowly. That question they asked was one I never anticipated. What worked, and what needs to be revised for next time?"

Comparing class outcomes with our original expectations is the key for reflection-on-action. Whether the lesson worked or not, reflection-on-action informs us of the need to revise our thoughts, beliefs, or actions in order to predict (and plan) more accurately the next time. This kind of reflection is crucial to good teaching, and the myriad factors at work in the room (student skills, our moods, the time of year, even the weather) mean that we are often reflecting, correcting, incorporating, and shifting as we go.

Schön's two forms of reflection are powerful teaching tools, yet I would venture to add a third form of reflection to his list: reflection-on-self.

Reflection-on-self brings thinking to a deeper level than the other two forms, for it asks us to consider *why* you planned the way you planned, *why* you made the predictions you made. It asks that you consider the beliefs that drive your behaviors.

For example, you notice that in your freshman class you frequently underestimate the time it takes your students to do any complex task. So you ask yourself, "What beliefs about my freshmen am I making? What developmental features am I ignoring, or do I have to learn to predict more accurately?"

Reflection-on-self is a challenging business because it is so deeply personal. It requires mental space, and it may lead to deep and fundamental change. This form of reflection asks, at a deeper level, how you approach teaching. Why do you call on the girls more than the boys? What is it about those poor kids that you find so frustrating? Why do you believe "those kids" are out to get you? Are kids really that different today than when you were growing up? When did teaching stop being "fun" for you?

To make these underlying reasons visible is to empower the learner. Once visible, you can then decide what to keep and what needs changing.

We are always teaching something; the big question is, what is it that we are really teaching? Are we teaching our students to be rule followers? Critical thinkers? Compassionate human beings? Good test takers? If we are unaware of the deeper learning lessons, we are held hostage to the unknown and to serendipity.

Powerful learning opportunities and experiences exist every day. Too frequently we dismiss or ignore those powerful opportunities and label them as "isolated events" or "anomalies," sighing that "they just don't understand." Holding a mirror up to our deepest thoughts provides us with choice. We can choose to keep doing, thinking, or believing as we currently do, or we can examine our strengths and weaknesses and choose what to keep or change.

For instance, have you ever heard one of your students say, "I hate this class?" Some students will, in fact, dislike any class. But, how many students have said that? Which students were they? Does how you are teaching the course have anything to do with that statement? Why might they say that? To ignore those comments is to miss a reflection opportunity.

They have reasons for saying what they say. Reflecting deeply upon the experience might begin a domino effect of change—one small thing at a time. You alter your approach and one child laughs. That laughter makes you happy and you talk more with other kids. They like being talked to and all of a sudden, laughter is part of your classroom.

As they laugh they tell you about their lives—and suddenly you realize you are teaching people, interesting people. Not "students," not losers, not mini-adults, but people who are doing the best they can, just like you. They need you to mentor them, to push them, to convince them that learning is a powerful tool for living in a changing world. And this all happens in small steps that you are aware of and control.

Story: When I was still a textbook-recitation teacher, I had a mother come in one day to talk about her son. She said that while he was not labeled as special education, he had some real issues with his ability to read, especially under stressful conditions. She was wondering if I might give him more time to complete his chapter tests.

I told her I would think about it, and I did. I thought: if I gave him more time, wouldn't the other students want more time as well? Was that fair to them—or was I just being equal? Even if I wanted to give him more time, how might I manage that? I could not give him more time right after class without robbing his next teacher of classroom time. And if I let him come in after school to finish, wouldn't he cheat and look up the answers in between? A hundred different issues arose in my head.

And then I thought, did I want to know what he knew . . . or . . . did I want to know what he knew in fifty-three minutes?

That mother's one simple question ultimately became my cathartic experience and helped me change into a more inquiry-oriented teacher.

Our behaviors are the manifestation of our deepest beliefs. You act congruently with what you truly believe. To choose to live as you have always lived, to think as you have always thought and act the way you have always acted, is to live your life comfortably. Refusing to look deeply into your personal belief mirror is to limit your own growth.

Sometimes looking in the mirror makes us uncomfortable because what we see is not what we had hoped for. We might see a lack of purpose and vision, a going along with the flow rather than reaching for our highest hopes. We may not know where to begin or feel trapped into our current patterns of existence. We may look and see ourselves as less creative, less risk-taking, less life-changing than we'd once planned. These are tough reflections to address.

Let's be clear: this is not a book about guilt. You are where you are and that is fine. Guilt emerges when you see the weakness in yourself and do nothing to change that thought, belief, or action. This book is meant to help you notice the reflection opportunities you have each and every day and if you choose, to take advantage of some of them for future personal growth.

Life begins anew today. We can always, at any time, choose differently. It is never too late.

There is a story about an old man who was talking to his gardener about planting an oak tree. The gardener mentioned the fact that oaks are slow-growing trees, thinking that his employer might realize that he would be dead long before the tree was mature. Instead, the old man said, "Then we haven't a moment to lose!"

Small steps lead to big changes over time, as long as you begin the journey. There is no guilt, no self-incrimination; there is only where you are right now. Reflection-on-self is all about possibilities. It is forward looking, not 20/20 hindsight. Reflection-on-self is about owning your own life through the choices you make on a daily basis. If you don't like what you see, make different choices and see what happens.

What you see in the mirror is always perfect—for a learner. Either it tells you how well you are doing—or it tells you what you need to change next. Either way, it is learningful.

NOTES

1. Simons, Daniel, and Christopher Chabris. "Selective Attention Test." YouTube video, 1:22, last modified June 19, 2012, http://wn.com/selective_attention_test.

2. Schön, Donald A. *The Reflective Practitioner: How Professionals Think in Action.* New York: Basic Books, 1983.

Chapter Two

Why We Do What We Do

(and Why They Do What They Do)

Middle school is not for the faint of heart. Students' bodies are changing as well as their hormones, thinking patterns, social interactions—everything all at once. The questions that consume our students start changing as well. Suddenly, perhaps in the middle of a fascinating lesson on earth science or world history, they begin grappling with such ongoing Big Questions as "Where do I fit in?" "Why do I look like this?," and "Why on earth did I just say that?"

Unable to hear those questions running through their heads, we wonder why they act as they do and why they seem so different today than they did yesterday. The only constant appears to be rapid change.

While middle school is generally recognized as a transition time, these big questions may stay with us all as we age and mature. Our personal grappling with these kinds of questions helps us understand and appreciate our students as they attempt to answer, "Why am I the way I am?" Our understanding and empathy for our students affects the way we interact with them, the way we set up lessons to reach them, and the way we approach classroom discipline.

ALL YOU NEED IS . . .

Do you believe that students are choosing to misbehave? This question is posed every year to teachers taking a Master of Education course, and the response is just about always fifty-fifty. "They can't help it," some of the teachers say, recalling past classes on child development or anticipating that it might have been a trick question.

"Yes they can," others argue, and they have ready examples of actions where the student certainly knew better. Eventually, they want to know who's right.

The answer is yes, students are choosing their actions, and for a reason: whatever actions they are doing are their best attempts to meet their needs at that time.

Imagine that a student, let's call him Mike, has not done his homework. Again. It's clearly problematic behavior, with consequences that will hurt him. The homework was assigned for a good purpose. Why would he choose not to do it, especially with his grade sitting where it is right now?

It depends on Mike's needs. Not doing his homework might meet his need for power, allowing him to say, "Don't tell me what to do!" Alternatively, skipping the assignments might allow him to avoid failure and save face, letting him tell himself, "I could do it if I wanted to . . . but I just don't want to." Alternatively, the choice might reflect his greater need for sleep, or better time management skills, and so on.

Our needs occur within a context, and students exist within far more contexts than a classroom. Any student of Psychology 101 has likely been introduced to nature vs. nurture, the debate that asks, "Are you the way you are because of genetics or your environment?"

Under the genetics argument, we can point to the strengths and weaknesses each of us is born with. We can say, "I am good at math, just like my mom" and "Everyone in my family has strong organizational skills." But, those in the nurture camp retort, are you good at math because your mom helped you or encouraged you in her favorite subject? How much does our environment encourage or inhibit our abilities?

The reality is that both influence us heavily. We are who we are because of our genetic predispositions as well as our experiences. That's what makes understanding the needs of students so interesting, so challenging, and so worthwhile. Any number of reasons could underlie a student's choice to misbehave or underperform (or, alternatively, succeed brilliantly). We make decisions to meet our needs at the time. And, because those actions meet our needs, we generally think those decisions are right—at the time.

Of course, just because an action meets our needs does not mean it was the best choice to make. Mike is clearly hurting his learning opportunities and his grade by refusing to participate.

Consider a far more serious example. Gangs meet their members' needs for love and belonging, but in a highly dangerous way. In order to keep fitting in with that family, to keep meeting that intense need we all have to belong, gang members make choices that are illegal, with serious long-term consequences.

From children to teens to adults, from safe to highly dangerous situations, several key needs control us throughout our lives. Different developmental theorists have tried to label those needs.

According Dr. William Glasser's Choice Theory, there are four basic psychological needs: belonging, power, freedom, and fun. The first two are social needs. Belonging is the need to feel connected, and power is the need to have others recognize what we do or say as important. Freedom refers to our need to think and act without restriction, to be individuals. And fun is the drive to laugh and feel good. These needs drive us, according to Glasser, no matter where we are.

Dr. Abraham Maslow approached the subject of needs from a different direction, formulating a hierarchy in his paper "A Theory of Human Motivation." He argued that humans are motivated by unsatisfied needs, and that we cannot move up his pyramid until the larger, more basic need below it has been met.[1]

Figure 2.1

Working our way up from the bottom, we will not care about living in a safe place, having job security, or ensuring financial safety nets (safety needs) if we are preoccupied with such basic physical needs as air, food, water, and sleep (physiological needs).

Once we have both of those covered, then we feel driven to belong to a group and seek out friendship (social needs). Once we find solid social support, we then work for recognition, achievement, attention, and self-respect (esteem needs).

Our needs motivate us to climb toward the proverbial mountaintop, with the ongoing search for Truth, Meaning, and Justice at the pinnacle of achievement.

What does this mean for the classroom? Students who are hungry and tired are not going to be primarily focused on learning. Ditto for students whose home life is uncertain or unsafe. Ditto for students preoccupied by their need for love and support. These students can and do learn, but other powerful forces are also competing for their attention.

In order to feel comfortable in our own skin and able to learn and be successful, we need the basic ABCs:

Autonomy—a sense that we are in control, that we have both power and freedom;
Belonging—a sense that we are loved and fit in somewhere; and
Competence—a sense that we are capable and good at something.

Much time has been spent discussing whose theory is best and how it should be organized. For our purposes here, let us simply say that the needs for belonging, love, power, and freedom are fundamental drives, no matter how you label or graph them.

Our students, juggling multiple needs, are going to use different words entirely.

Picture a young teen at the mall with his parents. You'll see the kid walking by himself, a good fifteen feet apart from his parents, doing his very best to pretend they don't exist. Two conflicting needs are going on here. He needs the safety of his parents nearby (as well, probably, as their money and a ride home), but he wants to be cool. He needs love and belonging from both his peer group and his parents, but he doesn't want to look like he needs them—at least, not while others are watching.

Ask him why he's behaving the way he is, and he might tell you how uncool his folks are, but he likely won't explain everything. He probably can't.

Most of us would be hard pressed to articulate the needs that drive us, even when asked point-blank. The more practiced we teachers are at identifying those needs, the more effective we will be at responding to our students. The goal is to be proactive, to help students address those needs in ways that will allow them to be good learners.

CRIME AND PUNISHMENT

A teacher is complaining about a difficult student. "I told the student twenty times not to do this," she says, frustrated.

Who's not learning here?

The behavior is working for the student in some way. The problem is that the teacher is doing the same thing repeatedly—saying "stop that"—while expecting different results each time. Maybe the student wants the attention or wants to get kicked out of class. Maybe the student's self-view is so deficit that to protect her own ego it's better to say, "I don't want to do it," and save face rather than risk failure.

As teachers, we have to be able to understand our students, what their needs are, and how they're best trying to meet those needs—all without them articulating their precise needs to us. It's a tremendous challenge, and every student is different. But if we cannot see what their underlying needs are, we are the ones who end up frustrated. What our students are doing is perfect for where they are (even though it might drive us nuts).

Happily, sometimes their needs change in a relatively short period of time and then so do their behaviors. They find the power they need or support from a new group of friends—or sometimes they find out that what is really bothering them is normal, and they are not the only ones wondering and asking that question. Sometimes patience can be a virtue.

If students knew another behavior that would help them to be more successful, they would probably substitute it. If there were a way to meet the need for power, or belonging, or anything else on the lists that theory gives us—without the negative consequences—they would likely choose that instead.

But—and here is what those graduate student teachers point out when they argue that kids "can't help misbehaving"—they may not know what else they can do to meet those needs. It's a new situation. Being told "don't do that" doesn't help the problem. What we need to say is "try this instead."

The question is, can you as a teacher figure out what that student's needs are and substitute that particular action with something better? Is there something else you can point the student toward that will safely satisfy those needs while making her a more successful student?

At the time of this publication, there is a national push to move schools toward a Response to Intervention (RtI) model in order to address the needs of academically and socially struggling students. This approach is particularly used for students who might otherwise be referred for special education or emotional behavior disorder (EBD), the goal being to keep the students in their mainstream classes if possible.

Response to Intervention takes an individualized, data-driven approach. The school psychologist and the teacher are both involved, keeping data on the behavior of the student in question and focusing on the factors that trigger the problem behavior. Armed with data, they can anticipate when Bailey throws a fit or Kevin disrupts class; the school psychologist and the teacher can then tailor a response that avoids that trigger or substitutes a more successful behavior.

Let's go back to our earlier example of Mike repeatedly not doing his homework. Let's say you talk with Mike after class, and after a few minutes of conversation it becomes clear to you that this is a power issue.

Your challenge as a teacher, then, is to figure out if there are other ways Mike can participate in class that might fill his need for power. Can he play to his attention-grabbing strengths by leading his group's next presentation? Can he be the one to pass out papers? Might the next paper assignment be broad enough that he can choose a subject he feels strongly about?

Wait a minute, you might be thinking. Some of these suggestions sound like rewarding bad behavior. It sounds like Mike here is getting too much power.

As the adult in the room, you should be able to differentiate whether a situation is a power issue for you or not. You are ultimately the one in charge, the one who enforces the rules and determines the grades. There are clear lines. However, there are many situations in the classroom where students can make choices and even have a bit of power without threatening your authority. As the adult, you are the one who is best able to step back and look at the situation long-term in order to determine what is best for each of your students to learn.

After all is said and done, Mike is still the one who chooses whether or not to do his homework and participate in class. He might choose not to, no matter what you do. There is no method of teaching that will ever result in every single student learning and succeeding, if a student chooses not to put in the effort.

What about punishments? What about rewards? They have their place, absolutely. Yet, after considering the complex needs that drive us, punishments and rewards represent a fairly shallow level of understanding people's needs.

If you say to a student, "If you do this, this bad thing will happen," what do they learn? For some, the threat is enough to eliminate the behavior. For others, they learn not to get caught. Talking of punishment in this way does not give students an alternative. After all, what if the student doesn't care about the promised punishment? If detention or copying the dictionary or failing the class, and so on, no longer matters to the student, then what are you going to do? If punishment is the only option in your disciplinary bag of tricks, then you are stuck.

What about rewards, then? Alfie Kohn, in his book *Punished by Rewards,* argues that punishments and rewards are different faces of the same coin. Both state that "if you do this, this will happen"—a form of conditioning so basic it has been used on lab rats for decades. There is nothing wrong with getting stars or praise or pizza parties, but these incentives quickly teach us that the promised reward, and not the learning process that gets us there, is where our focus should be.

A reward system, when it is the only behavioral system in place, supports the idea that people deserve to be rewarded for doing good things. Whether they should be or not, the reality is that the real world is not fair in its bestowal of recognition and success, no matter how deserving we might be. Rewarding good behavior feels much more positive than punishing bad behavior, and it can at times be effective, but you as a teacher are still left with a shallow "if this, then that" approach to discipline.

A deeper level of discipline, then, is understanding. It begins and ends with asking, "Why are you choosing to behave this way? Why does this make sense for you?" Given all the needs that can motivate a student at any given time, you as a teacher need to be able to respond in ways that are just as varied. You can choose to use punishments and rewards, but now they are no longer the only choices you have. Chapter 4 will go into power and discipline in more detail.

VISION ADJUSTMENT

Most of this chapter has looked at how our students view the world and what needs drive them. What about us? The truth is that it's easier to spot what drives another person than it is to recognize the lenses through which we see the world.

Every person has his or her own mental model, his or her own lens through which he or she views the world. Religion, gender, or politics are all examples of mental models. These may be structures we have chosen, or we may have grown up with them without even realizing. Mental models are not good or bad in and of themselves, but models of which we are unaware hold us prisoner.

If you are unaware that you are holding a particular mental model, it controls you. You behave in ways that seem to make sense to you—in alignment with your mental model—unaware of what other options there might be.

Story: I began my teaching career as a traditional textbook-recitation teacher.
That was what I had experienced for 99 percent of my schooling life, what I
had seen when I was in the school observing, and what my cooperating teach-
er modeled when I student-taught. When someone said "teaching," that was
the picture that popped into my head.

When I got my first teaching job, I relied on this textbook-based model on
a daily basis. I worked hard to write good exams, give interesting and dynamic
lessons, tell good stories, and become an effective teacher.

Looking at student test scores over the years, it began to dawn on me that
no matter what I did, many students failed. They did not "like" science. They
did not study. Even when I told them exactly what was on the test, they were
not motivated to give their time, effort, or resources to memorize what I told
them to memorize.

As I began to look for alternative ways to reach my students, it dawned on
me that I was being held hostage by my beliefs about what science teaching
looked like. I would have to find a different model of instruction if I wanted to
be as effective as I dreamed of being.

Just like our behaviors, our mental models can change. It's hard, and it could
take years. Maslow would place these mental models at the top of his pyramid, the "seeking truth and justice" part that represents the highest level of
striving. We may or may not reach them. Still, once you know that those
models are part of who you are, they become changeable, if you wish.

In short, we and our students do what we do, think what we think, and
believe what we believe because it is what we know and what seems to work
for us. It meets our needs—or so we think. All of us could be more effective
in some area of our lives: relationships, school, job, career, health, happiness,
spirituality, balancing the multiple demands we find ourselves in. Reflecting
upon our choices is a gateway to a more self-actualized life, for you and your
students.

NOTE

1. Project Management Course. 2012. "Maslow's Hierarchy of Needs." Abraham Maslow:
Father of Modern Management. Retrieved from http://www.abraham-maslow.com/
m_motivation/Hierarchy_of_Needs.asp.

Chapter Three

The Power of Learning

Did you ever cram for an exam? Picture it: the late-night study sessions, repeating over and over the facts that you suspect are going to be on the test. Perhaps you come up with mnemonic devices to help the facts stick. Fueled by coffee and anxiety, you memorize the material so that you can walk into the exam room and regurgitate what you know.

Two days later, when the class is done and the exam is being graded, how much of that information do you remember?

What did you actually learn?

People frequently confuse good memorizers with good learners. In fact, most school classrooms view them as the same thing. Many people believe that if you memorize well, you are very smart. You show it on the recall tests and get good grades. Homework is no big deal to you because you like memorizing vocabulary words, dates, places, and notes from class. You are very good at what it takes to be a successful student.

Memorizing well may help with what we know, but it does not determine what we are able to do with those facts.

Learning in its most basic form is defined as a change in thoughts, beliefs, or actions. *Change* is the operative word here—in order for learning to take place, some thinking or behavior has to be different after the learning episode than it was before. Achieving that change involves trial and error, practice, resources, effort, time, and commitment.

Reflection (at all three levels) is involved. And that makes learning a personal choice. Some people might be able to force you to memorize things (if they have something you want, such as a grade) but only *you* decide what you are going to learn. Only you decide what you are going to integrate into your thoughts and beliefs, what you are going to allow to influence your actions.

People outside the school setting are, generally speaking, pretty decent learners. They can learn how to drive, cook, have sex, keep their jobs, navigate new technology, and interact with others. They learn what they need to learn in order to meet their needs. They seem to find friends, find jobs, make a budget, raise children, and deal with both successes and failures.

Life, it seems, is not so much about memorization as it is about learning. The more a class focuses on the latter, the more relevant the lessons will feel to students' lives.

Likewise, while people who learn tend to have a strong knowledge base, knowledge is less about the accumulation of facts than about what we do with them. Facts are the "food for thought," not the thoughts themselves.

Knowledgeable people are able to make meaning from their store of facts. They connect new information with what they already know, what they value, and how they think things work. They decide whether and how the new information fits. They can access that new information more easily, because it has been connected into their overall system of thoughts and understanding.

Other words that demonstrate deep knowledge are *insight, interrelationships*, and *interconnections*. All of these words focus on the idea of connecting facts to something else. Interrelationships and interconnections focus on precisely how the pieces or facts are related to each other and within a whole.

Facts in isolation—say, a list of vocabulary words on a page—aren't very useful. Put those facts in context, and suddenly we can start noticing connections and relationships. Suddenly those facts are doing something. They matter. When we grasp the context, when we see the overall pattern, and that pattern allows us to intuit the facts, or to know where to look them up. The more we can draw connections, the deeper the learning.

Memorization might get us through the test, but deep learning sticks—long after the class is over.

Say, for example, that you are teaching cell structure and function in a high school freshman biology class. The facts associated with this lesson are the names of the cell parts and what they do: their structures and their functions. If students only learn to label a diagram of a cell, then they are learning those facts in isolation.

Making meaning of those facts, by contrast, requires the students to consider how the parts interact, and how each cell structure has its own function, which directly impacts other cell functions. Cells are integrated wholes, systems unto themselves that exist within larger systems. Knowing this system allows students to connect what they are learning at the microscopic level with other, larger systems at play in the world.

Imagine having just taught a chapter on cell structure and function and trying to assess students' learning. On the chapter exam you give the following task: "Relate cell structures to their functions." One of your students responds, "Cells are a lot like cars"—and then goes on to explain the cell using a car as an example. He explains about the fuel, the computer, the wiring, the exhaust, the doors, the windows, the ventilation, the spark plugs, and so on, and everything is connected to the working of cells.

Eureka! That student has fully integrated knowledge of cells into his own understanding. He can label the parts, but more importantly, he understands how those parts are connected and is able to recognize that pattern in other situations.

Many teachers state that their favorite part of teaching is watching their students "get it." Few things are more rewarding than watching that exact moment of insight when new knowledge is made. When that "aha!" moment happens, we know we are doing something right—something lasting for student learning. Isolated items are now connected into a meaningful whole.

RISK AND FEAR

When you come upon new information, it can do one of the following: 1) support what you already know, 2) modify your current thoughts, or 3) cause you to reconsider how you view big and important things. The last learning experience is by far the hardest for it causes you to *re*-think, *re*-view, and *re*-prioritize your past thinking and experiences. It is like going from being single to being married, or from being childless to being parents—everything changes in how you think and what you think you know.

Learning, then, is a risky activity—which makes it fun and exciting and scary and fearful and nerve-racking. It is the pre-performance jitters, the sweaty hands, the adrenaline dumped into your bloodstream—it is what performers live for and the rest of us cope with.

It is high-risk because you cannot go back to the way you were. You have been changed: you have new knowledge, new beliefs, or new skills. You see the world differently than you did before.

What kind of classroom climate is best suited for encouraging this risky activity? The Affective Continuum gives us a useful scale for considering learning environments. This scale is particularly helpful for designing learning in a classroom with a variety of skill levels. As seen below, fear and boredom sit as opposite ends of the spectrum.

Fear_____ Attention_____ Comfort_____ Boredom_____

Take a moment and check off where you, personally, would rather be as a learner. Are you best motivated when you're relaxed and comfortable? Sitting on the edge of your seat? Where do you estimate your students are along this spectrum?

Research shows that maximum learning, depending on the person, takes place somewhere between fear and attention. Fear of failure, when it becomes overwhelming, can cause us to freeze, but get us too comfortable and the drive to discover lessens for many students. No one likes to be bored.

The challenge for teachers is that, in a classroom of varied abilities, one student's "attention" is another's "bored." Knowing the relationship between these emotions can help you vary the pace for your students.

One place where the shift from one part of the continuum to the next is crystal clear is a school theater production. There are days when it feels like there is plenty of time until the show. The students relax into their roles, not worrying if they have to call for lines. The director has the script in hand, a form of safety net if they lose focus. There is time to goof off.

As opening night approaches, however, the attention sharpens. There's an urge to get it right, and that hand gesture or voice inflection that was fine a month ago suddenly is the subject for director's notes. Then tech week comes, and invariably, there is a rehearsal where everything flops. The cues are sloppy, the acting is flat, the energy is low. The show looks awful.

Fear strikes students and director alike: what if this is the worst production ever? Parents are coming; tickets are sold. There's no choice but to muscle on through. With cast and crew perched somewhere between Fear and Attention, they make the play fully their own, and the show finally pulls together.

In theater, you might catch kids worrying aloud about whether the play is going to be good, but in the classroom, you will rarely hear fear expressed. Think about it: how often have you heard someone say, "I'm afraid I can't do this?" Probably never, and if you did, I'm willing to bet it was not in front of a group.

Fear is not cool. And for people who are constantly wondering "where do I fit in?," who have an important need for love and belonging from their peers, expressing fear is not a good option. It *is* okay, however, to express boredom. That's socially acceptable. No matter how effective of a teacher you are, "this is boring" has probably passed through someone's lips.

Fear and boredom may be on the opposite ends of the continuum, but when students try to explain their feelings, the two are closely linked. When students complain that a class or subject is boring, it does not necessarily mean that they are bored. It might mean they are afraid of failing, that the risk in this particular assignment is too high. Fear may cause them to disengage, which leads to boredom. Or, they may not want to take the social risk of saying how they feel.

Knowing the Affective Continuum helps us teachers modulate the pace and risk level of our learning activities so that as many students as possible can have those moments of insight. Understanding is about far more than correct answers on a memorization test. Our goal is learning, and learning changes us.

Powerful learning opportunities may ultimately lead to self-actualization. You begin to own your own beliefs in the face of many choices and to possess a repertoire of skills, as well as the faith that you can learn new ones if needed. Learning that is clear, explicit, and valued becomes a powerful life tool and an antidote to the fear of change.

Chapter Four

Working *with* Students

A Collaborative Approach

When we talk about working collaboratively with students and allowing them to own their own learning, let's be honest: what we're really talking about is power. Who is going to control the power in the classroom and to what purpose?

Power permeates all human interactions. Generally speaking, teachers have power over students and, by extension, over most parents. (See Chapter 17, "Including Parents/Guardians.") Teachers are on par with other teachers, though they tend to have less power than administrators. There is a hierarchy in the classroom and in the school.

If students have power, then teachers don't. Right?

Not necessarily.

It depends what kind of power we're talking about and how it's being used.

The Power Pyramid, often cited in psychology and education textbooks, makes clear that there are different kinds of power in a given situation.

1. Coercion is probably what people think of when they think of power. Coercion is raw control over someone else. It is the power of punishment: the stick and the dunce cap in classrooms of old. Coercion says, "Let me use your car or else."
2. Reward is the power of getting. It is the carrot dangled in front of the donkey to keep him moving. Reward says, "Lend me your car, and I'll give you something good in return."

3. Title is the power of respect for the position someone holds: parent, teacher, principal, superintendent, president, and the like. Title says, "Lend me your car because I'm your mom."

4. Relationship is the basis for a mutual give-and-take kind of power. Stephen Covey in *The 7 Habits of Highly Effective People* describes relationship power in terms of an emotional bank account. Each person makes deposits into the relationship, and those deposits allow for later withdrawals, such as favors or extensions of grace. As with a bank account, you must contribute before you can withdraw. A relationship that involves only taking is not solid. Power that comes from relationships says, "Hey best friend, can I borrow your car?"

5. Understanding is the power of knowledge. Rooted in reason, this form of power gets results because everyone understands why the end goal makes sense. Words such as *purpose, relevance,* and *shared destinations* come to mind with this form of power. Power that comes from understanding says, "Lend me your car because you don't need to use it today, mine is in the shop, and I have to get to an important doctor's appointment (please)."

Most schools run by coercion and reward alone in order to get students to behave. In fact, the whole student handbook could be seen as a form of coercion; it clearly outlines the punishments students will receive for various inappropriate actions. Schools express the power of reward through such incentives as class rank, grades, and recognitions like student of the year. Some schools reward good class behavior with pizza parties or school bucks to be spent at a concession stand. Extra recess is a reward; the loss of it, coercion.

Teachers used to hold tremendous power derived from title. The teacher had ultimate control (supported by coercion) and was deserving of complete respect because he or she was the teacher—period. In much of the world, this continues to be true. Informal American culture has led to a weakening of this form of power, particularly in older grades, although the principal still tends to hold power of title.

Still, some hierarchy remains in the classroom. You are the teacher and mentor, not the students' friend. This separation allows you to be the giver of grades and consequences, as well as the encourager.

The more the power in your classroom is based on relationships and understanding, the more smoothly the class will run. These forms of power are based in equality and respect, which means they do not need to be enforced through discipline.

Story: One of my favorite quotes is, "A good use of power is to empower others." It speaks to putting others in positions where their needs will be met. It speaks to making yourself dispensable, and it also speaks to human potential.

To grow competent, compassionate human beings means to use power in ways that are not so distinctly self-serving. It means that you are learning how much power you need (not just want), and that takes practice and reflection. Power is not good or bad, it just is.

The Power Pyramid becomes particularly interesting in terms of communicating grades to students. Coercion says, "Keep doing that and it will lower your grade." Reward says, "Do this and your grade will improve." Title says, "Here is your grade, handed down from on high because I am the teacher." In each of these examples, the student may or may not understand how the grade was derived, and he or she certainly cannot question it. If the student does, he or she will be seen as a bad student who challenges authority.

Power derived from understanding says, "Let's talk about what you have learned rather than your grade." The trust that comes from relationships assures students that the grade was earned, not given according to whim or favor. Rubrics are excellent tools for communicating grading rationale and thus build understanding.

The key to working *with* others, rather than over them, is to have relationships and understanding as the primary modes of power in your classroom. These forms of power allow for more flexibility in the classroom. You can share the power with students, depending on the task, without losing control of the classroom. How you use power depends on the task, the student audience, and the way you view your role as teacher. The Power Pyramid, at the very least, is a reminder that there are options.

RULES AND REGULATIONS

Do it because I said so. Because that's the way it has to be. That's how it's always been.

What are these statements really teaching children? Such statements rely on title power, with the promise of coercion or reward to enforce them. These statements are not based on understanding. The teacher is telling the student what to do without explaining why. Certainly, teachers do not have to explain themselves for every little thing they do, particularly with young children. But, again, what are these statements teaching?

When you're in a rule-following environment, what you are learning is to follow the rules. Let's start by asking a few questions about these rules.

Who benefits from the rule following?

Do quiet classrooms really translate into more learning—or do the adults just like it quiet? What about seating charts? Why memorize facts students could look up on their iPhones?

Do we really want to grow a generation of rule followers—people who just do what they are told because we tell them to? If not, then at what point are we hoping our students will make the switch from obeying to thinking for themselves?

The problem with most rule following is that it is imposed upon others without giving them voice. There is no power, freedom, or choice in the matter. Some students will follow blindly and some students will rebel in this situation; neither case leads to a classroom of self-actualized individuals.

Some rules absolutely make the school a safer, friendlier environment for learning: great! Other times, rules simply reinforce one person's power. If you understand why the rules exist, then you have some flexibility on when to enforce and when to bend them for the sake of student learning. Which brings us to:

What learning is actually taking place when we focus only on rule following?

Are students learning to follow the rules, or are they learning not to get caught? Are they learning not to trust adults, to do what they are told even if it doesn't meet their needs? What about might makes right?

If the only form of power that students see is power over others, then they stand a good chance of copying that strategy. Power over others: that sounds a lot like bullying. If rules appear to students as if their main reason for existence is to keep the power structure intact, those same students might make the same kinds of rules when they are in positions of power.

Rules designed to maintain the power structure do not lead to change or allow for powerful learning. They lead to a rigidity of thinking where the list of rules and consequences grow year by year.

> *Story: When I was a high school teacher our school had a student handbook. It listed all the rules and the levels of consequences for each infraction.*
>
> *And every year it got longer and bigger because every year, students found loopholes that they exploited to the maximum. Teachers would say, "That's against the rules," and these students had done so much studying of the handbook, they knew exactly what was not forbidden.*
>
> *So every year, more rules had to be added!*

Let's be clear: there is absolutely a time and place for following rules and behavior plans, but it shouldn't be all the time, and it need not be your first and only option. There will still be assertive discipline, detentions, and naughty behaviors no matter what you do. If you need to write a behavior contract to help a child change his behaviors, do it. The more long-term intent is to help your students become more independent, self-actualized humans, not to fear adults or hook them on extrinsic motivations.

When reward and punishment are used as a blanket approach to all class-room behavior issues, there are both intended and unintended consequences to those choices. It might look like the following example.

Picture a naughty class on a day when nothing is working. Let's say one student, Riley, has been mouthing off, and three or four other kids are taking cues from that behavior. As the teacher attempts to get Riley under control, others lose focus; Bailey is sleeping in the back and three others have their phones on their laps and are texting not-so-secretly.

"That's it!" the frustrated teacher says, trying to keep order before the room starts bouncing off the walls and the chairs start flying. He pulls out the big guns. No recess. Field trip canceled. Pop quiz time. You will all have essays on my desk tomorrow morning on the deadliest subject I can think of. Et cetera.

In this scenario, perhaps one-third of the class is misbehaving, whether they are trying to disrupt or simply seizing an opportunity. What about the other two-thirds? They have just been punished because others were bad. What are they thinking about the fairness of their teacher right now? What are they thinking about certain other classmates? All sense of community has long since flown out the window.

When everyone suffers because of what Riley and a few others started, an environment is forming in which students learn to tattle on him, to ostracize him until he starts acting the way they want him to. What a poor choice of power! And it's not teaching Riley the right message, either.

The reverse is also true. If two-thirds of the students are behaving, they don't need rewards to ensure that behavior. They are already doing it.

What kinds of rewards should you use for those students who need positive incentives? It depends on the students. Because the reward—like the punishment or the rules—is for them, not you. If the reward you've always relied on does not seem to be working, consider: do you want to use the bait that you like or the bait that catches fish? The better you know your students, the better you can estimate what reward will be enough to help them want to change their behavior.

Punish and reward the students who need it. But ultimately, the goal is to change the culture of the classroom to one where coercion and reward are not the mainstays, so that when Riley gets an attitude you have additional options available. That shift begins when you think less about rules and more about values.

THE SHIFT FROM RULES TO UNDERSTANDING

While rules insist upon certain behaviors, values focus on the social norms we follow so that we can learn together most effectively. Values are modeled through understanding and relational power, never coercion or reward. They develop over time, and they last far beyond the school year.

> *Story: When I was working on my doctorate I spent about 100 hours studying "self-esteem"; who had it, where it seemed to come from, what types of circumstances seemed to lead to developing it best. I finally left the topic because I did not think I could help students change their self-esteem in the one semester timeframe I was working within.*
>
> *I did learn a lot. The one idea that has really stuck with me is that kids who grow up in households where the expectations are consistently enforced are the ones with higher self-esteem. It appears that when they know where and what the limits are, they begin to connect their choices with success and failures—they begin to own whether they are successful or not.*
>
> *Clear and consistently enforced expectations seem to be the key.*

The way to see whether rules or internal motivation regulate student behavior is simple: what happens when the teacher leaves the room? If the teacher is the only one keeping power and control, then when the teacher leaves, chaos ensues. The naughty kids seize the advantage, and the ones who love order try coercion: "Come on, you guys, we're going to get in trouble!" It pretty much never works.

And when the teacher comes back in the room, what happens? Exactly what the good kids promised.

On the other hand, if students act a certain way because they want to (it meets their needs), then they will continue to act the same whether you are there or not. In a classroom based on relationships and understanding, the class as a whole decides upon the social norms by which it will interact. Students come up with the rules of engagement as well as the enforcement for breaking those rules. There is still order, but in this case everyone knows how that order came to be.

One way to get students thinking about these social norms is to ask a question like, "What makes someone your friend?" Students will come up with a list of the usual suspects, such as respect and honesty. A more interesting way to get at the same values is to ask the opposite question, "What is something you could do to totally destroy that friendship?" The qualities of a good friendship align with the qualities of a highly functioning classroom.

Once the class has come up with its description of good behavior, the teacher's question, then, is this: "Are you expecting me to *make you* do this? If so, you are putting me in the role of the enforcer."

A question like this allows you to reframe the conversation about discipline, clarifying that it's not about you punishing or rewarding students. Rather, it's about students living the life that they want to live as effectively as possible. If they are disrespectful, people won't want to work with them.

Coming up with class rules is not about how students will be punished, but rather how they will start to choose more appropriate behaviors. After all, the goal is not for students to be polite because you are enforcing it. The goal is for them to respond politely because they are courteous people. By asking these questions, the discussion switches from the importance of following rules to the possibilities of becoming self-actualized.

In order for this approach to be effective, decisions concerning classroom climate have to be made *with* students, not by the teacher or school alone. That means that students have a choice; they must be able to see the issues as relevant to their lives and their needs. In a classroom based on the power of understanding, it's helpful to discuss how hard it is to change a pattern of behavior. Talk about how changing habits is difficult, and use a reward system as necessary to help students change it. Focus on your forward progress.

As with learning, students must see the behavior as important to themselves and their quality of life in order for anything to change. They must have appropriate support as they change their pattern of behavior.

Not only are you helping your classroom to run more smoothly, but you are preparing students to become participants in a democratic society. In both the classroom and the world, there is a delicate balance between what is best for the individual and what is best for society as a whole. For people to own their behaviors, especially within a society, it is best to have them understand *why* it matters to manage their own behaviors.

PARADIGM SHIFT

In all reality, saying we're going to work *with* students rather than making them do what we want is a huge paradigm shift. Certain things are no longer possible. You cannot see students as empty vessels waiting to be filled with your knowledge if you want to work collaboratively. In that model, what do the students have to offer but their rapt attention? Recognizing what students bring to the table is the first step in this paradigm shift.

Working *with* students requires a needs-orientation, a learning focus, and a developmental understanding. Having a needs-orientation means constantly keeping in mind the students' perspective. You take students' hierarchy of needs into consideration in both planning and teaching. What will they recognize as helpful for their future?

The goal is always student learning. Having a learning focus means keeping your eye on that big picture. How can you orient your classroom to best allow students to change their thoughts, beliefs, or actions—based on what they are learning in your class? Your students own their own learning. They are the ones who choose what they will remember and whether it will change them.

Having a developmental understanding means that your expectations are grounded in an understanding of how your students think right now. What are they capable of right now, at this moment in time? Children and teens are not mini-adults, as Chapter 8 on setting appropriate expectations will discuss. If you cannot connect with where students are right now, you cannot work with them as effectively as you might wish.

What does that look like in the classroom? Let's have a look at five specific actions that teachers can take in order to help them work with students. Later chapters will keep expanding on these ideas.

1. Talk about the learning journey.

We teachers can talk all we want with each other about how learning is a journey, but if we do not have that discussion with our students, they will be left out of the loop. Take time in class to address, specifically, how what you are learning in class will meet their needs. By connecting it to their lives today, you build their commitment for the tough times ahead.

As you talk about learning and reinforce that with your actions, plan to use ideas from each of the power levels discussed earlier. Different students will understand different parts of the Power Pyramid. Some will learn from failing and redoing their work (coercion), some from getting a well-earned good grade (reward), some from being specifically directed by the teacher (title), some from a communal "we" focus that allows for creativity and individuality (relationship), and some from understanding why their learning matters (understanding).

2. Observe with a purpose.

Look for strengths and weaknesses in ability. Find out who is good at what, and make those students your classroom experts for that task. Watch for where students are having trouble so that you know what to teach next, either to the whole class or to a specific small group that you form to the side.

Watch their actions to see which skills (or errors) they are repeating (and, in doing so, cementing into their understanding).

Listen to find out where they are right now. Ask them about their visions of the future, for themselves and the world. Find out what they already know, and incorporate it into your discussions.

Watch to see how they treat others so that you can recognize their beliefs. Engage them in creative activities to help them become willing to consider other points of view, other ways of doing things, other ways of thinking and knowing.

3. Choose an optimistic point of view.

Choose to view your students through the lens of "they are doing the best they can." You will have students who prove otherwise, who lack motivation. Do not let that optimistic lens falter because of a few individuals.

Students need help replacing ineffective patterns with more effective patterns. As we'll talk about in the next chapter, replacing those patterns is hard work that requires strong motivation and appropriate support.

You are dealing with a rapidly changing audience with shifting needs who do not understand what is happening to them. Those physiological changes are outside their control, and talking about them is key to understanding them.

Your students need:

• People who empathize with their changing selves.
• High expectations (in spite of those changes).
• Multiple opportunities to contribute.
• Safe opportunities to fail (so they can learn).
• People who like them for who they are—right this very minute.

Remember, they are perfect as they are; they are just growing and changing.

4. Make the criteria for your teaching choices visible.

Your students cannot read your mind. Tell them and show them what you want them to do and why. Use a "think aloud" strategy to model what you want to see. This includes the who, what, when, where, and why features of your lessons. Post your expectations in your room as a banner and reference them daily.

Be explicit about how your classroom is relevant to their lives and futures. Tell them, "Today we're talking about x, and what you're learning will help you with y." Don't assume they'll make that connection for themselves—that's very high-level thinking.

5. Hold everyone accountable.

In order to succeed, students need consistent, high expectations for learning and behaviors. Make behavior expectations explicit (rubrics help) and learningful (rather than punitive). Use the type of power that is most learningful rather than the easiest. Coercion and reward are the easiest, but they lack depth and understanding. When you do use them, make sure the consequences are as clear and consistent as the expectations.

Every individual in your classroom is on a personal learning journey, conducted in the company of others. As you honor and celebrate that growth, allowing students more freedom as they show they are capable of handling it, working *with* your students will become more and more natural.

Chapter Five

Practice Makes . . . ?

Have you ever heard the expression "practice makes perfect?" It's the quip we throw at the team before they run the drill again, at our kids when they complain about homework. People who thought that statement was true told it to us. Actually, it is incorrect.

Practice makes permanent. Only perfect practice makes perfect.

The point of practice is to develop a habit, routine, or pattern of behavior. Through practice, the new pattern becomes so firmly lodged in our minds that we can think about other things at the same time. Through practice, we no longer have to focus attention on breathing correctly while playing an instrument, conjugating verbs in a foreign language, or calculating basic arithmetic as part of a complex math equation.

Skills are what first come to mind when most people consider appropriate subjects for practice, but that only reaches the surface level. Knowledge and even disposition issues can all be changed through purposeful repetition, as long as we're willing to put in the work.

Practice takes time, effort, and frequently resources. In order to cement the new skill or knowledge or belief, we need multiple repetitions, and we need to be focusing on each and every attempt, rather than simply going through the motions. We might go through a mountain of clay before that first cup or bowl comes out of the kiln looking like something we'd want to own.

None of these descriptions of practice are new. But, practice it wrong, and that new skill becomes even harder to learn correctly.

Story: I had a neighbor once whose name I mislearned. It was Gary, but somehow I got it in my head that his name was Dave. Don't ask me how. I lived next to him for over five years and every time I saw him I had to think like this:

I want to say "Hi Dave!"—but his name is not Dave.
His name is the same as your wife's brother's name.
His name is Gary.
"Hi Gary! How's it going?"
That's kind of a complicated process just to get one name right, all be-
cause my initial practice learning his name was wrong. Until I was solid on
his name, I wasn't likely to move on to the next step of getting to know him
better.

Practicing with permanence in mind turns your classroom feedback, a "past" orientation, into feed-forward, a "next time" orientation. The quality of your comments matter, because they are influencing a new pattern of action, information, or way of viewing the world. With your responses, you are explaining to students why it is necessary to practice at all. You are clarifying what pattern you are trying to help them embed.

And, because the learning builds on itself throughout the course, you can link this pattern to the next level of learning that will be expected later. You are showing how understanding this formula makes tackling the next big question possible, how mastering this verb tense opens up new lines of conversation. Perfect practice is necessary—and rewarded—at every step.

More than simply drilling a new skill into someone's head, practice breaks down big tasks into bite-size chunks. Organized appropriately, it makes complex or unmanageable tasks possible to achieve.

Think about when you first learned to drive a car. You lifted your foot off the brake, stepped on the gas, and suddenly this multi-ton vehicle was moving at a threatening speed, with only you to control it. In that first moment, the idea of merging with seventy-mile-an-hour traffic seemed an impossible feat. (And if it didn't to you, it probably scared the heck out of your parents.)

Driving a car is a huge, complicated, complex process—hence driver's education. Hence months and months of careful practice, starting in an empty parking lot or on a quiet road—music off, cell phone off—building up confidence and motor skills (pun intended) until driving feels like second nature.

The real test of how correctly and thoroughly we've practiced comes when pressure gets turned up. When we merge onto the highway or encounter slippery conditions, we revert back to what we know best, revealing the patterns that are most embedded within us.

In a teaching or coaching situation, then, it's okay—it's good—to put students under pressure in order to find out what their fallback patterns are. Debriefing the results afterward can give students valuable reflection time on the purpose of practice.

OLD HABITS DIE REALLY, REALLY HARD

As with relearning a neighbor's name, any pattern can be replaced with a new one—if you're willing to put in concerted effort. The more deeply embedded the current pattern or habit, the more time, effort, and resources it takes to replace it with something new. Old habits die really, really hard: complex habits might take two years or more to replace. If the habit is tied to a physical dependency, as with smoking or other substances, inserting a new pattern becomes even more complicated.

Complicated, but possible. The key point here is that you have to *want* the new pattern more than the old. The new pattern you want to achieve has to more closely meet your goals for yourself (your needs) than what you are currently doing.

> *Story: I used to play pool every other week with my father-in-law and six other guys. Of the eight people, six of us smoked cigarettes. When I decided to quit, I promised myself a reward—a new motorcycle jacket—at the end of one year of being a nonsmoker.*
>
> *I still to this day remember standing in that basement, pool cue in hand, having an internal argument with myself. "Go ahead and smoke, you can start a new year tomorrow." "Just smoke one—you don't have to tell your wife. She'll never know." "Just breath deep; there is so much smoke in the air you don't even have to really light one up."*
>
> *Smoking while playing pool with those guys was a deeply ingrained habit. On the other hand, I really wanted that new jacket—enough to change my pattern of behavior and finally quit.*

The same is true for any new habit you strive to create. You have to want it more than what you are currently doing. The "want to" has to be greater than the "now."

What habits are your students learning as they strive to be successful in your class? Are there any bad teaching habits you possess that you might need to relearn?

HELP ALONG THE WAY

Learning a new pattern usually involves plenty of failures, frustrations, and setbacks. Therefore, there is a delay in acquiring new patterns. Whether we are learning a new pattern for ourselves or trying to help our students do so, acknowledging these challenges helps to set appropriate expectations for the learning road ahead.

It helps to acknowledge—out loud, in class—that difficulty and failures are part of the learning experience. Achievement would not be so fulfilling without the struggle. It helps, too, to provide emotional support and encouragement to keep learners from giving up. As a teacher, your careful feed-forward and content expertise ensures that students practice the new skill correctly from the start—saving valuable time later.

During those times when the going gets slow, it helps to keep a long-term view of the "new pattern learning" process. Keep focused on how this new pattern fits with what you want to achieve. Whether you are learning an instrument, rehearsing the school play, building assessment into your teaching practice, or pushing your students toward that next big breakthrough of understanding, keep focused on the quality of life that the new pattern will allow.

You've seen the weight-loss ads and TV shows that astound the audience with their "before" and "after" pictures. In any area where a new pattern is being learned, evidence of "before" and "after" can be powerful motivation. Focused on the task ahead, we learners easily forget how far we've come. Pausing to reflect on our progress makes explicit what is worth celebrating.

When students see improvement, that builds trust—both in themselves and in their teacher's ability. Every action that builds trust is like making a deposit in an emotional bank account. When a teacher says, "I know this doesn't seem relevant at the moment, but trust me, you'll need this soon," it's that account students are drawing from.

When learners compare their figurative "before" and "after" images, they are able to celebrate their individual changes and achievements. They can see how the learning has changed them. They can make comparisons with themselves and judge their growth. It's a far more freeing approach than comparing themselves with others to see who is best.

It's easiest to spot the fruits of our labor when we're practicing a specific skill or action. When we can do something that we couldn't do before, that's satisfying. Still, those skills only become important or relevant when they can be seen as part of the whole. Most skills are not important unto themselves but because they allow you to do a part of the bigger task. The clearer that big picture, the more motivated learners will be to practice the skill in the first place.

Consider the way math is taught at the elementary level. Certainly this depends on the teacher, but adding and subtracting are often presented as isolated skills. The tasks come with little or no context, and the goal is to correctly complete a page of problems. Some students will find satisfaction in being able to finish a whole page, but others will quickly come to wonder why they need to do *another* work sheet. What's the point?

There's no denying that adding and subtracting are important skills, but what makes them important is their relevance to our lives. If you use cash to make a purchase, these skills matter. If you are measuring, building, or baking, addition and subtraction matter. They matter because they allow us to do something relevant and important. And they are the first steps to being able to do some really cool higher level math. Context gives skills relevance. The practice needed to get those skills right is worth the effort.

More challenging to change than our skills is our knowledge. While knowledge has facts as its foundation, true knowledge deals with the complexity of how those facts are connected to each other and to other content. To be knowledgeable means you know the facts and also see the patterns within the facts. At the deepest levels of knowledge, patterns within one content area are seen as modifications within other content areas.

Practicing new knowledge and patterns of thinking requires more time, effort, and resources than learning a new skill, and it's harder to spot when we've achieved deep understanding. Practicing new knowledge is not simply about accumulating new facts, *Jeopardy!* style. Rather, evidence of successful practice comes in changing how we understand the world around us.

Hardest and most time consuming to change are our beliefs, those deeply implanted concepts about how the world works and why. They are so difficult to change because for the most part our beliefs are invisible to us, and therefore seem like common sense. Of course every five-year-old needs to be in school; of course schools have summers off; of course school needs to start early in the day; and of course administrators should make more money than the classroom teachers. Really, of course?

Everyone has their beliefs, and those beliefs impact how you think about the world and others around you. For students, many of their beliefs are reflections of their life experiences and their parents' views. "Before" and "after" views of their beliefs require a safe learning environment and a willingness to look beyond the norm and to what could be. Beliefs can change, but only through a personal commitment to time-consuming, focused effort.

Given the time, effort, and resources it takes to learn any new pattern, practice needs our careful consideration. We need to ask ourselves—and clarify to our students—the point of practice. Why is it worth everyone's time and effort to get it right?

> *Story: When I started teaching science as inquiry, I had my students complete these sheets called Idea Evaluators. Students had to identify appropriate criteria for that specific decision, then rate their idea choices using those criteria.*
>
> *One of my students, in particular, hated those Idea Evaluators. Every time we did one he would loudly voice his opinion about how worthless he thought they were—and this was after my explaining how they related to his life outside the classroom setting. He just did not see their value.*
>
> *The next year he stopped by for a chat. He was hanging his head when he shared with me the following experience. He was quite a good football player and had in fact received four college scholarship offers. He went and visited each campus, met with the coaching staffs, and talked to other students. His problem was that there was so much information he just couldn't decide.*

So, head hanging low, he told me that he got out one of the hated Idea Evaluators. It allowed him to explicitly name what he was looking for and what he valued most.

As we practice, we are developing new habits of mind as well as new actions. Most important is the habit of reflection, which allows us to look back on where we've come from and how our learning has changed us. Practicing the habit of reflection, we can see ever more clearly where we've been and where we want to go next.

Chapter Six

Teachable Moments and Safety Nets

Frustrations and Failures as Learning Tools

Consider any action movie that you've seen recently. Chances are excellent that the plot of the movie fits the hero myth. A normal, run-of-the-mill person is given a quest that requires stepping far out of his or her comfort zone. Supported by a safety net of friends and mentors, our hero faces a series of obstacles that slowly transform him or her from a nobody into somebody worthy of our admiration. Learning has changed him.

Then there is a moment when our character considers the risk of failure to be too great, and the audience fears the worst. The hero has to reach inside himself or herself and draw on what he or she has learned throughout the movie before he or she can defeat the bad guy, win the admiration of the love interest, and generally emerge victorious. There are a number of variations on this plot, of course, but the point remains: we learn and change when we face challenges.

Learning involves risk. There is a reason those lessons we learned through trial and error stick with us so deeply; they involved the real possibility of messing up, and there were actual consequences for failure.

If we truly want our students to learn and be changed by that learning, our classrooms cannot be risk-free. Learners need the risk of failure. They need to have the opportunity to realize what they do not know and have that need motivate them to learn.

And yet, fear of failure makes many people afraid to act. Rather than facing the social, emotional, or academic consequences of failure, learners may give up. They may decide they've always hated that subject, or they may stick only to the safe territory where they know they can succeed. Risk and the chance of failure, in and of themselves, do not automatically lead to learning.

How do we as teachers create those moments where students realize their needs while still maintaining a positive atmosphere? The answer lies in creating safety nets.

> *Story: My teenage boys had a curfew they were to follow when they were out with their friends. That curfew was specifically set up as a safety net for them. They knew I would be up when they come home. They knew I knew what alcohol smells like.*
>
> *No teen wants to look uncool in front of his friends, and it can be hard to resist peer pressure. My sons were responsible for making good decisions, but having a curfew allowed them to make good choices and pass the blame off on their parents. "I can't—dad will be up when I get home." I certainly didn't mind being the bad guy in this case.*

Many of us build safety nets into our curricula and simply call them by different names. Low-stakes assignments, drafts, and redo options are all safety nets. They all have something at stake; they are all assignments that require students to put in work and end in teacher feedback. Yet failure in that assignment does not lead to a failing grade in the class. Instead, poor drafts create opportunities for revision, which lead to better final results.

The skill of a teacher is in finding those teachable moments, those moments where students want to learn because they have realized they need the information in order to succeed.

TEACHER AS SAFETY NET

Consider structuring a classroom to offer information on demand. The idea is that you do not need to know everything up front; you only need enough information to keep you going, to help you reach the next step.

Computers, for example, can do a vast array of projects, but that doesn't mean we need to know how everything works. We don't need to know programming language to check e-mail. When programming language (or any program) becomes necessary, we'll figure out how to use it or seek someone who can teach us. Not before.

Imagine a project where students have to give a presentation. They gather their materials and consider what they want to communicate. But how do they communicate it? In trying to answer the question, students will first consider what they already know. They may already have the answer from a past course, and this assignment gives them a chance to apply that past learning in a new way, further cementing it.

Alternatively, a member of the group might raise her hand and ask, "How do I make a PowerPoint presentation?" She may have never cared about using that program before, but now she needs to know, and she is ready to learn.

That is a teachable moment. Student interest is higher and retention is greater because you as a teacher are equipping students with the tools they know they need. The definition of a professional teacher is one who can answer the same question fifty times in a day with as much enthusiasm the fiftieth time as the first: because it's the student's first time needing to know.

This process of letting the students ask the question first can be a challenging transition if you are used to a classroom where the teacher lays out all the tools up front, where questions either mean the students weren't listening or the explanation wasn't clear enough. With that state of mind, it's easy to view student questions as a failure on our part to make the assignment accessible.

Because we want to prepare our students well, our tendency is to attempt to equip them with everything they might need. "Sometime this week," we tell them, "you're going to need to know this." That approach may work well for some students, particularly those who are motivated to learn in general. But for others, the front-loaded approach is an opportunity to zone out mentally. Until they have the question in their head, the information is meaningless.

Letting the questions drive the lesson does not mean that the class is out of the teacher's hands. Teachers can control those teachable moments. The sign of a master teacher is one who can set up learning in such a way that he or she knows, without a doubt, that in the next fifteen minutes of the lesson students are going to ask this question. Students have a sense of risk: they may or may not be able to figure out the problem on their own.

Where do safety nets fit with all of this? For students grappling with a project or a calculation or a challenging text, their safety net is knowing that when they need help, they can ask you. The relationship you have with your students is well enough established that they know they can ask questions and trust that the answer is available. The challenge, as a teacher, is letting the students ask the question.

It's a fantastic teachable moment, not a failure, when students working on a project approach you and say, "I don't know how to do this." Rather than giving them the complete answer, it might be appropriate to say, "I don't know either, but here are resources. Go find the answer, and then you tell me."

What you are communicating to your students is that you trust them to figure out the answer for themselves. They might feel frustrated. Without feelings of frustration, there are no feelings of celebration. Without the frustrations and sometimes failures, there is no powerful learning.

One of the keys of teaching is to make yourself dispensable. If you do your job well, the students won't need you by the end of the year. Or, they'll need you to be very different than you are right now. The relationship after a year's worth of work should look different: your students have been changed by their learning.

STEPPING OUT ON A LEARNING LIMB

Students come into the classroom believing, knowing, and being able to do certain things. From a learning standpoint, that is where you must begin. Start new units by asking students, "What do you think you already know about this concept, this idea, these facts? How do you think these things work together? How are these parts connected in your minds?"

Beginning with what students already know is a fundamental safety net of learning. It grounds them in prior learning rather than assuming that no one knows anything. Therefore, it is a strength-based idea versus a deficit model.

This learning safety net is termed the "re-" model, for it asks students to re-think, re-vise, re-learn, re-view, and re-do what they already believe, know, and can do—with more complexity, more facts, and more sophistication. It requires that they bring their prior experiences to the learning table and use them as a base for their future learning.

Think of trapeze artists learning their craft. Their safety nets literally save their lives. When they start out, they probably need that safety net regularly. As they learn and excel, they need it less and less. But it's still good to know it's there.

CONSEQUENCES

A safety net allows students to take risks, fail, and try again within the age-appropriate limits that the teacher has devised. It does not mean that it will prevent all students from failing. Drafts and redos are excellent options, but if students do not take advantage of them, or do not learn from the feedback they receive, they can still fail.

> *Story: When I started teaching, I would rail at my grade book as I calculated final grades. If he had just come to school more often, if she had just handed in those assignments that I had asked her for, I wouldn't be forced to assign this failing grade.*
>
> *Still, I felt guilty, even when the grade was the clear, inevitable consequence for their choices. Passing them would not have helped them learn the material, nor would it have taught the larger lesson about responsibility in future classes.*

Most adults (parents and teachers) hate failing, and we certainly don't want to watch others go the same route. We feel that failing is our fault, not the learners'. But here's the rub: when you save kids from failing, you save them from powerful learning opportunities.

And it's hard. Whether you are talking about the classroom or life, it's hard to watch someone stroll boldly past our carefully constructed safety nets and fail—especially when we've made the same mistakes, when we know the answer, and when (as we do) we want the best for them. It's hard to watch others struggle. It's hard to watch them make the same mistake many times over before they finally get it. The thing is, we need the struggle in order to learn.

It's easy to give advice. As parents and teachers, we've been there before, and we really can help. Our intentions are great. But making decisions for kids does not help them learn. If they don't see the connection between choice and consequence, how can they possibly learn to be responsible?

Here's a scenario that's probably familiar to any parent or teacher living in a cold weather climate. It's time to go outside, and your kid doesn't want to put on a coat. "But I'm not cold!" he says. It's perfectly warm at the moment, he reasons; why should he bother?

As an adult, you've had plenty of experience with cold weather, including not dressing warmly enough, and it's easy to save him from the cold by ordering him to put on his darn coat. A power struggle ensues: your will against his. Can you picture the argument?

Let's go back to the idea of safety nets. You want him to learn, and a few moments of cold might be that perfect lesson. That said, you also want to protect him in any way you can. And so, you give him a choice: "It's thirty degrees outside and it's windy. You can either put on your coat now, or you can carry it with you."

The learning opportunity is there, but the safety net is that he's got the coat in his hands (or you're carrying it, depending on the child's age) when he realizes he wants it.

The kinds of struggle, the number of choices, and the level of the safety net all change depending on the age and maturity of the student. With younger children, the safety net is going to be clearly visible, and any punishment happens immediately. We tell them, "You know that when you steal crayons, you get a timeout."

With older children, the consequences can be more serious, and they are mature enough, developmentally, that they can wait a few hours or days while we formulate the proper response to their actions. We are communicating that the consequences are the logical and loving result of poor decisions.

The *Love and Logic* series offers excellent age-appropriate examples of teaching children through choice, empathetic responses, and clear consequences—more than this chapter could possibly cover.

As students at any age come to trust that that you will provide the safety net, they are free to explore and get creative, to venture into new learning territory. That is the subject for our next chapter.

Chapter Seven

Living in a Changing World

The Complimentary Roles of Creativity and Critical Thinking

Here is a wonderful definition of insanity: doing the same thing over and over and expecting different results. We can all smile at the image of a kid opening the cookie jar repeatedly in the hopes that cookies will appear, or groan at the college student's time management decisions that lead to yet another all-nighter, but how often do we repeat the same steps over and over, thinking, "Will it work this time"?

If you've taught the same class more than once, you've probably walked into class with a lesson and realized partway through that it didn't work very well last time, and this time is shaping up to be the same. You'd meant to fix it, but then there were those assignments to grade, and that meeting, and so on. Sometimes you walk into the class knowing that the lesson could be better, but how?

The solution requires both creativity and critical thinking.

We are often taught to think of those two terms as being as far from each other as you can get. Either you're a creative person, or you're analytical. Right?

Wrong. Creativity and critical thinking are two sides of the same coin, and you need to give your full attention to both, in turn, to have success as a teacher or a student.

Creative thinking might ask, "Are you willing to think of alternative answers for how to approach class? Can you turn off your internal editor, let your imagination run wild, and come up with boatloads of ideas, not worrying about how good they are?" If you allow time to delve fully into the creative process, the result is a fuller, more interesting lesson plan than you might otherwise have come up with.

Critical thinking might ask, "What criteria will you use to decide which of those one hundred ideas works best for your classroom?" Critical thinking in this case considers time, materials, class atmosphere, and other factors. It involves seeing through the eyes of your students: if I were seven or twelve or eighteen, what would matter to me?

Take these two tasks from a student's point of view, as the student sets about trying to arrive at a topic for a research paper. The first idea that springs into his or her head may not be the most interesting or original paper topic. But, if the student is required to brainstorm thirty possible ideas before doing anything else, something on that list is bound to be interesting.

Then—and only then—can he or she begin to think critically about these topics. What is the length requirement? Can he find enough information on this? Can he write about it objectively? Does he really care enough about this topic to spend the required hours on it?

Here is a fun exercise that demonstrates to students just how important and accessible creative thinking is.[1] This exercise was designed to prepare students for research projects, but it can also be adjusted to get them thinking about how things work. Put students in small groups of three or four and hand them an everyday object about which they must generate a full sheet's worth of questions that might be worth researching. Make the objects as everyday as possible: a pencil, a fork, a plastic bag . . . whatever you have lying around.

When students run out of their initial ideas, challenge them to think outside the box, considering the object through historical, environmental, philosophical, sociological, and the like, lenses. Have them think about how they work and why. The groups then circulate the room, reading each other's lists and putting a check mark next to each question that could prove worthwhile to research.

The point of the exercise is that any subject can be interesting if you look at it from the right angle. Students surprise themselves with the ideas they can generate. It's amazing what excellent research projects can stem from a plastic bag.

Such activities, which benefit from having as many creative minds as possible working together, are excellent tools for a diverse classroom. Much of the talk about diverse classrooms uses language like "incorporating" or "accommodating" diversity, as though it were an extra burden to juggle. Rather than approach it from that direction, craft situations where people see that diversity is useful and necessary.

If you have students working in a group of five, for example, try to structure assignments so that it will be in everyone's best interest to partner with the four people who seem to be the most different—together, that group will have the most creative ideas. Diversity in all its forms becomes an asset in this valuable approach to learning.

TAKING TIME TO DO IT RIGHT

In both the class planning and paper writing scenarios above, it's important to note that creative thinking comes first. This process does not tend to work well in reverse.

There are two common mistakes that keep us from accessing and applying our best ideas. In the creativity stage, the mistake is cutting off the creative process too soon. Being creative takes a good portion of class time, much of which is spent getting past unoriginal ideas, but this time is valuable. In a list of one hundred, only two or three ideas will be truly unique and creative—and chances are very good they won't be among your first fifty ideas.

Try challenging your students to come up with thirty-five ideas within a given topic. They will groan at the large number, but given time, they will come up with a list. The next time, raise the bar to fifty. (It's Mickey's Whining Rule: the whining will be the same no matter what the number is, so make it a big number. And, they can do it.)

By the end of the semester, coming up with one hundred ideas won't be a problem. Students become more creative over time because they have learned that they can come up with as many ideas as they need to. They learn that they are creative, and that is an excellent use of class time.

The second common mistake is to skimp on the critical thinking. If you're a person who can generate creative ideas all day long, your challenge might be to spend enough time evaluating your ideas according to the important criteria. When you have more ideas than you can handle, how do you select the two that work best for your needs? How do you (or your students) articulate those choices?

After your students come up with their list of thirty-five, or fifty, or one hundred ideas, the next solid block of class time would be devoted to teaching the critical thinking they need to choose the best ones. Such work would involve evaluating requirements, examining their own skill sets, and exploring the criteria set up by your particular field of study.

Students learn to explain and defend their choices at a far deeper level than "because I like it." It's no longer a whim or serendipity that determines their project topics or controls their choices. Now rational decision-making is at play. Making those decisions is empowering!

Both creativity and critical thinking continue to be important throughout the lesson, not just at the start. Once your students have arrived at their essay topic, for example, they need creativity to find research and draw connections, and critical thinking to evaluate their sources. They need creativity to craft their sentences and their argument, and critical thinking to make sure what they are saying is well said. On and on it goes.

Knowing both creativity and critical thinking helps students be more confident in their decisions. Both sides are equally important, not only because they help create a good paper or a good lesson plan, but because they prepare students for . . .

THE REAL WORLD

In Chapter 3, we mentioned the pitfalls of strict memorization. Memorization involves accumulating facts, but real learning makes connections between those facts and involves change. In a classroom where the goal is memorization, there is no room for creativity—or critical thinking, for that matter. Students might spit back the facts for the test, but that approach to learning does not mirror the way life works outside the classroom.

They say that kids in school right now are going to have seven different careers before they retire. Some of them may not have even been invented yet. Having a good memory is a helpful feature, but being a good memorizer does not prepare you for success in this kind of world. Creativity and critical thinking do.

There is a strong correlation between people who rate themselves highly in creativity and those who see themselves as self-actualized. Those thinking-outside-the-box skills—and they are skills that can be developed like anything else—might help people to imagine more options before them and feel more in control of where they are headed in a global market.

Likewise, being able to identify the criteria on which to base our judgments can take a lot of the uncertainty and stress out of those life decisions.

The myriad judging television shows popular in the 2010s, such as *Dancing with the Stars, American Idol, Project Runway,* and the like, are perfect examples of just how emotional deciding on that criteria can be. An audience member might watch the stars dance and think, "Hey, that was great!" only to see the same performance picked apart by the judges based on elements we hadn't known to look for.

The judges are the experts—ideally—because they know the criteria for determining excellence in their fields. Those criteria can vary, which is probably one of the reasons those shows have a panel of judges. The reason the judges disagree, or the reason we yell at our TVs, is that sometimes different people have different criteria. When the judges change, the show can change dramatically.

An effective critical thinker, an expert in his or her field, can communicate to others which criteria he or she is using for each decision and why that criteria is the best for that specific judgment.

One of the major challenges we face in the Real World, particularly outside our fields, is not knowing the criteria. Consider all the decisions that go into purchasing a house, for example. Particularly if you're a first-time buyer, it's hard to know which criteria will turn out to be the most important. Should we pay more attention to the age of the roof, the size of the kitchen, the colors of the walls, the price?

If you are making a joint purchase with a spouse, articulating which criteria should get the most weight can be a huge challenge. Furthermore, the factors you look for when searching for a house are different from what the appraiser or inspector will focus on. When all the information is in and all the emotions have been weighed, it's those critical thinking skills that will ultimately allow you to make your purchase and be confident in the result.

Whether you are planning a lesson or buying house, one factor remains the same: if you know the criteria, you can make better decisions more frequently. You are able to say, "At that time and place, knowing what I knew, I made the best decision I could."

Even so, we all find ourselves looking back on our decisions, thinking, "If I knew the criteria then that I know now . . ."

And that is reflective learning.

NOTE

1. Ballard, Bruce *The Curious Researcher*. New York: Pearson Longman, 2010.

Chapter Eight

How Much to Expect?

Setting Appropriate Expectations

Kindergarten teachers can do magic tricks.

The teacher stands in front of her students and asks them to identify which is her right hand. Then she turns around and asks them the same question. The five-year-olds all point to the hand on their right side, the same as before. "No, this is my right hand," she says over her shoulder, waving at us. Her right hand has switched sides!

She does the same move several times, holding up her hand as she turns. Each time they are amazed that she can switch her right hand to what is obviously on their left, just by turning. It must be magic! The kids can't understand how she did it because, developmentally, their brains cannot grasp that concept yet.

Or perhaps you've seen this one: show a group of four-year-olds different-shaped glass containers, all with the same volume. Pour water from one to the other, demonstrating that they hold the same amount. Then, ask the children which one has the most water. They will point to the tallest one, every time.

You can explain and pour water back and forth until you are blue in the face, but those four-year-olds will not be ready to grasp the conservation of mass. Developmentally, they are not ready yet. No amount of good teaching will make them ready, until they are.

It's easier to talk about not being developmentally ready for certain tasks when we talk about young children, though of course that development continues in shifts and spurts for decades. The human brain undergoes a complex series of rewiring between ages twelve and twenty-five, far longer than we once thought.

Knowing that a major rewiring process starts around age twelve sounds about right because that's when kids in the United States are in seventh grade and their brains seem to disintegrate. Certainly, there are exceptions. But suddenly, many can't stay organized, even when they could in sixth grade. Adults around them find it frustrating, but it's a physiological thing that happens to them. Not a choice. In eighth grade, they're like amnesia victims, remembering that they used to know how to do that, whatever it was . . .

As adults, having gone through our own individual processes of developing and having (happily) forgotten large portions of the experience, when we're watching students at their various developmental stages, often it's a short wait before the "shoulds" come out. He "should" know better. She "should" be able to do that by now. "Should" expresses obligation, turning the above statements into responsibility issues.

The October 2011 issue of *National Geographic* ran an article on the teenage brain as its cover story, pointing out that teenagers weigh consequences less heavily in their decision-making process—particularly when peers are watching. The article speculates that the risk-taking that results has evolutionary benefits, pushing young adults out of the safety of their homes and into an expanding new world. That's helpful to know, but hardly enough to stop adults from shaking their heads and worrying when they hear of their teen's latest exploit.

Given the range of changes that are going on in our students, particularly after the age of twelve, how do we know whether those "shoulds," those benchmarks, are developmentally appropriate? In a classroom with a range of learners, how high do you set the bar?

GROWING IN SO MANY WAYS

Young kids are not mini-adults. They are at a different place than adults, developmentally, and they are perfect where they are.

Whenever we use the term "developmentally appropriate," we are talking within a three-year window, more or less. "Normal," therefore, covers a pretty big range. Consider all the dimensions development entails, as summarized by the acronym PIESM:

Physical development—physical growth, eating, sleeping.
Intellectual development—how we process and access information. For instance, is your thinking concrete? Abstract?
Emotional development—how we feel about ourselves. This can include our sense of self-efficacy, competence, and pride, as well as our response to successes and failures.

Social development—how we act around others. Oftentimes social and emotional development get labeled as maturity. Our social development also occurs within a cultural context; what might be normal in one culture, such as eye contact or physical contact between genders, could be inappropriate in another.

Moral development—our moral development refers to our sense of right and wrong, our sense of justice and fairness.

People do not develop equally across all five dimensions at the same time. You could have an intellectually advanced student who struggles with how to handle herself among peers, or an emotionally and socially successful student who is behind intellectually, and so on. In fact, if you were to create a visual representation of each of your students' developmental levels, you'd probably choose a Venn diagram, with each dimension of development shown as a different-sized circle overlapping the other circles by different amounts.

Development is not consciously controlled. Rather, it is mostly genetic in nature, and it is hormonally driven. In other words, development is a function of body chemistry, and we don't have a choice over that. Our developmental levels (PIESM), all together, have an impact on learning, reading, writing, behavior, sense of right and wrong, thought patterns, friendships, sleep, hygiene, expectations, and frustrations—just to name a few.

And each student in a classroom of fifteen or twenty-five or thirty-five is at a slightly—sometimes dramatically—different place.

Until you know what your students are capable of doing, you cannot have developmentally appropriate expectations. If a student is not developmentally ready, he or she cannot do the task. Period. If a task requires abstract thinking, for example, and the student has not developed the ability to conceive of the world in abstract ways, he or she will not be able to complete the assignment. It does not matter what method you use. (When the student is developmentally ready, however, then that method does matter.)

Let's face it: schools are generally not developmentally friendly places. They start and end at prescribed hours that may or may not fit the students' sleeping patterns. Individual Education Plans (IEPs) can be tailored to fit the needs of individuals with learning disabilities and other special needs, but those are the exception, not the rule.

In general, given full classrooms and high emphasis on accountability, schools expect that students should know this information by this age. Mandatory state testing assesses that progress according to firm guidelines. And though the people who design state testing are well educated in developmentally appropriate benchmarks, one does not need long in any classroom to know that one size does not fit all.

What is a teacher to do? We do not want to hold back those who are developmentally able. On the other hand, pushing students too far ahead of what they are developmentally ready for can be problematic, making the students feel like they are being set up for failure. The more regularly we fail, the more we expect to continue to do so. We become frustrated.

And while some frustration is necessary in learning—there is little celebration without the struggle—constant frustration creates trust problems. We may no longer trust that the people in charge want us to learn or are working in our best interest. Our need to feel competent is not met. Feeling powerless, we learn that learning is no fun.

It's a difficult, delicate balance that leaves you room for plenty of creative solutions.

SPIRALING UPWARD

The key is to have high expectations for students but to allow many ways to get there. Kindergarten and first-grade teachers as well as middle school teachers are masters at understanding kids undergoing a wide range of developmental changes, learning to be fluid with changing expectations. Just because a student is not ready now does not mean she won't get there next month.

It's okay to *introduce* students to ideas they will use later in life, even if they're not fully ready for them. Working with students where they are *will* prepare them for the future. It is not okay to prepare them for the future with little to no regard for what their capacities are now. As for students who are highly motivated, treat them as you would gifted and talented students, trusting that their drive to learn will keep them engaged along the journey.

Structuring your curriculum for spiral learning is one way to address a wide range of learning abilities.

A spiraling curriculum is structured around the big ideas (central concepts) of your field. In every field there are between four and seven big ideas that all its disciplines share. For example, in the field of science, there are the following disciplines: biology, chemistry, physics, and earth and space science. There are of course subdisciplines, especially at the higher grade levels.

Some big ideas in science are: energy, equilibrium, systems, and structure and function. What that means is that each of those big ideas is found in every discipline. Take the idea of energy. They talk about energy in biology (photosynthesis, cellular respiration . . .), chemistry (activation energy, bonding . . .), physics (motion, light . . .), and earth and space science (erosion, fusion . . .).

Therefore, in spiraling learning, you begin by asking students what they already know about energy (or another big idea)—and then use that information as a jumping-off point for future learning. How is that energy generated? What does it allow? What does that look like, exactly?

The big idea acts like Velcro for all the specific facts. All learning is organized around that big idea, and it is taught over and over again, each time with more detail and with more complexity.

As you continually move deeper into the material, you are constantly spiraling back around to key concepts and information, viewing them from new angles and at new levels. For some students, that third time around might be the moment where it all clicks together. For others, returning to those key concepts allows them to integrate them more fully into their understanding; the fact that you are always moving forward allows them to make new connections, rather than feeling stuck in review.

Using that spiral model keeps both the teacher's and the students' focus on increasing understanding rather than increasing the number of facts students know. Memorizing facts might feel and look like learning, and certainly it's easier to test, but knowing more facts does not equal long-term learning.

Developmentally appropriate rubrics and criteria, handed out with the assignment if possible, are a helpful communicative tool and a great grading timesaver. Using a rubric with clearly stated expectations, arranged in levels of complexity, allows students to reach those learning goals in different ways at different times.

They can start off the school year, for example, competent in analysis, needing improvement in organization, and excelling in making creative connections. Such multilevel feedback makes it clear to students where they excel and where they need to go.

Be aware of your audience and the range of where they are likely to fall on the PIESM list at the start of the chapter. Are they growing physically at this point in time? If your legs hurt because your bones are growing faster than your muscles, concentration on some days might be difficult. Ditto if you're worried about getting that first period. These are not reasons to slow down the class, but keeping them in mind might help you feel less frustrated if students absorb that learning the second spiral around, instead of the first.

Are they concerned about dating, driving, needing to wear deodorant? Some of those developmental concerns might make their way into your classroom discussion. It's not a poor use of class time, because they are already thinking about these things, anyway.

Two caveats before we move on. One: there is a difference between not being developmentally able to do a task and not wanting to do it. This chapter is not an excuse for a lack of motivation.

Two: development flies in the face of many parental and adult expectations.

Development is not a race. There will always be some parents who push kids to grow faster. Yet, in a world where our students will likely stay in the workforce longer than we or our parents did, why rush? Children need time somewhere in their schedules to play and be happy. Isn't that what we all say we want for our kids, for them to be happy? Given time, clear expectations, and their own motivation, most students will get there.

The goal of this chapter is not to give you concrete lesson plans, but to help you reflect and adjust, as necessary, the way you approach your classroom. The way you think about your students and the expectations you set—that's one more pearl in your collection. The specific lessons that you end up incorporating into your classroom will be truly your own.

Chapter Nine

You Think That's Funny?

Humor as a Teaching Tool

Good teachers engage their students and inspire them. As teachers in the habit of reflection, no doubt you have thought back to your favorite teachers throughout the years and tried to figure out just what made them so amazing. Was it his passion for the subject? Her way of making learning fun? His knack for making you look at the world in a new way?

A 2004 study compiled the top "teacher qualities" based on surveys of more than three hundred students.[1] The list reveals a balanced combination of personality traits, knowledge of content area, and instructional skills. Their top 7 teacher traits were as follows:

- Approachable
- Knowledgeable
- Enthusiastic
- Encouraging/Understanding
- Effective Communicator
- Creative/Interesting
- Respectful[2]

The ways a teacher demonstrates these traits are wide and varied, but what's striking when you look at this list is how many of these traits are communicated through the use of humor. A teacher who can make his or her students laugh is perceived as approachable and accessible, for what is more humanizing than telling a funny story? Humor might reveal a teacher to be enthusiastic, understanding, and interesting. And some forms of humor can communicate ideas wonderfully, or at least put the listener in a place to be receptive to them.

Humor is a high-risk activity for both the teacher and the students. It is not simply the fear that the joke will fall flat, although twenty-five so-not-amused faces would certainly be enough to scare most people away from a second attempt. (Although there is certainly something humanizing in a failed joke . . .) Done wrong, humor could come across as offensive. Certainly, you don't want to get a laugh at the expense of a student, unless you know with complete certainty that that student will appreciate the joke and the attention.

On the other hand, research shows that humor in the classroom increases student learning. Humor is a highly creative endeavor that can be used to grab students' attention, help them remember ideas, and allow them to demonstrate deep understanding.

One of the most powerful gatekeepers between short-term and long-term memory is emotion. It does not matter whether the emotion derives from success or epic failure. Positive or negative, funny or sad, such emotional highs allow the associated memory to go virtually unimpeded into long-term memory.

Through the gentle buffer of humor, teachers can put a positive spin on stressful subjects or open up new lines of dialogue. They can label the stressor without pointing fingers and provide a way for students to learn from other people's mistakes. Humor can release the tension in the room, allowing us to laugh and let it go.

Story: I have a teacher friend who tells the following story about himself. He was doing a workshop presentation to a school faculty. He is a rather intense person, and he was very much into his presentation. One of his quirks is that when he is presenting, he also has a tendency to put his hands in his pockets and then rock back and forth on his feet.

So, he is presenting and explaining and connecting with his audience when all of a sudden, over the school speaker system, he hears his name being called down to the office. Well, needless to say he was more than a little peeved. Who would dare to interrupt him during his presentation? Didn't they realize how rude that was? What about his audience—he had them totally paying attention to everything he was saying. They had their eyes glued to him, and then he has to go to the office.

He makes it to the office in a less than happy state of mind, where the principal informs him that his zipper is down and he could not think of any other way of telling him.

When he tells that story, I laugh so hard it makes my eyes water and my sides hurt. I can see it as if I were there and feel it as if it were me!

There are so many ways this story can work in a classroom to alleviate fears about public speaking, to demonstrate the importance of not jumping to conclusions, or to let students know that everyone makes (and survives) embarrassing mistakes!

THAT'S NOT FUNNY (TO ME)

It's worth clarifying that, when we talk about humor, we are not simply talking about being joyful in the classroom. You might have a naturally sunny, happy disposition, and that might be how you communicate your enthusiasm for your subject. Great! If this description does not naturally fit your personality, that's just fine. You don't have to be cheerful to be funny.

Often when we use humor, we do so because we want to create a pleasant atmosphere and because, frankly, we want others to like us. Both of those may be positive byproducts, but let's look beyond that into classroom application. In this chapter, we'll explore how humor can be a teaching tool that you use to elicit specific responses.

There is no faster way to kill a joke than to explain why it's funny, but it's helpful, at least, to look at the reverse. Why does humor fail?

Humor is complicated and contextual. If you have spent time in another culture, communicating in a different language, you've seen firsthand how culturally based verbal humor can be. Some things are not viewed as humorous in some cultures. Religion or one's parents, for example, might be fair game for jokes in one culture and highly disrespectful in another.

Humor is also experientially based. A funny thing might have happened on the way to the forum, but if your students can't relate, they won't care. Some situations are only funny if you've been there.

Likewise, the experience being described needs to be stressful enough to keep our attention (A gorilla walked into a bar? What's next?), but not so stressful that you can't laugh about it. After the World Trade Center attacks on September 11, 2001, *Saturday Night Live* did not air a show until September 29. Rudy Giuliani, then the mayor of New York City, appeared on the show, and the cast asked him for permission to be funny again. (His response: "Why start now?")

So, too, some things are funny at certain ages. (Knock-knock jokes, anyone?) Watch any animated movie in a theater filled with parents and kids, and you can instantly tell which jokes were aimed at which age group. The adults smirk at the innuendo, included specifically to keep their attention. Let a character get his pants pulled down, revealing boxers with hearts on them—now it's kindergarteners who are giggling.

We can say, then, that humor is audience-specific. For something to be funny, it is best to have some shared experiences or at least some similar experiences to draw upon. The listeners need to be able to imagine themselves in the same situation that is being described. The better you know your audience, the more effective that humor will be.

ALL KINDS OF FUNNY

The goal is not to turn a teacher into a stand-up comic. But, if humor is an approach you naturally turn to anyway, it's worth considering how different kinds of humor might help engage your students.

Jokes work in a similar way to stories. You set the scene with a particular time and/or place—the more details, the stronger the story aspect. Then comes the rising action, which builds toward the climax. You have to provide enough of a story to put listeners in that time and place, make them feel the stress in the situation and believe they know the logical ending.

Instead of a climax, you get a punch line. The ending is different than the listener predicted. The stress that built up is now relieved.

Humor, then, is grounded in creativity. It's seeing something from a new perspective that makes us laugh. It's recognizing a pattern and applying it to a novel situation. Explaining the connection between jokes and stories can be a great way to help older students connect with the elements of a story, particularly if you are asking them to do some writing of their own.

Of course, there is more to humor than jokes and funny stories. Here are some other examples that might find their way into a classroom.

Physical humor, like tripping, falling, crashing, getting hit, and general slapstick, transcends language barriers. *America's Funniest Home Videos* has made a fortune with this type of humor. You see kids jumping on a trampoline, or someone skiing peacefully down a slope, and you just know something bad is going to happen. As long as the person is able to walk away at the end—with bruised pride, perhaps, but nothing broken—we can laugh.

Exaggerations and tall tales amuse us by offending our sensibilities. "That's not possible!" we say, smiling.

Cute stories aim for a reaction of "awwwww;" sometimes that's just what we need.

Puns might make your students groan and roll their eyes, but they have their place. Puns play on vocabulary and require control of language to understand.

References to funny pieces of pop culture can be a great way to engage students and draw connections, provided it's pop culture that students recognize. Parody takes that reference to the next level by placing the reference in a new, more ridiculous situation.

Innuendos suggest multiple interpretations to our words (if you know what I mean). If you're not paying attention, you'll miss the joke. Do make sure the joke is rated classroom-appropriate.

Bloopers—when generally competent people just plain mess up—are great for a quick laugh. Typos, grammatical errors, and word misuses that thoroughly (and amusingly) changed the meanings of student writing can be a fun way of underlining the importance of proofreading work. Have students keep their eyes open for funny examples from the paper and local signs.

Still other approaches catch us by surprise in an amusing way. Whether it's voicing a new perspective on a common experience or hearing someone put into words what you never thought they'd say out loud, these various shades of humor are all tools in your teaching toolbox.

A note of warning: sarcasm does not work in the K–12 setting. Students do not see it as funny, and it is too easy for a student to feel hurt. Those satirical or ironic comments may sound witty, but all too often sarcasm is saying mean things under the guise of humor. If you use humor of any sort in the classroom, be prepared to talk (and apologize) when you attempt to be humorous and offend people instead.

LAUGHING IN CLASS

We've mentioned several kinds of humor, but what matters here is how you use them. What does humor allow you as a teacher to do? Here are four ways that humor can be useful in your classroom:

1. Breaking the tension.

    Humor is great for breaking the ice on the first day of school or waking up sleepy students at the start of class. An amusing story at the start of a lecture, a relevant comic slipped into a PowerPoint—these techniques, used well, can garner goodwill and keep listeners' attention.

    Alternatively, humor can also be a life-saving technique after an intense discussion. Perhaps you have been teaching a particularly dark topic, and you are making the choice to relieve some of the tension in the room before switching to a new subject. Perhaps a student has just revealed an awkward or difficult experience to the class, and you are looking to take pressure off that student.

Doing something irrelevant or unexpected can help relieve that tension. Jokes, puns, or physical humor can change the mood and get students focused on a new topic—just make sure that your humor *in no way* invalidates the serious experience that has just occurred.

2. Locking it into memory.

Humans are genetically predisposed to listen to stories. Students who will tune out a lecture will generally still listen to a story, particularly if it's funny. Claim someone else's story as your own if you need to, and take your time setting the scene. The more fleshed out and engaging a story is, the less likely it is to feel like a vehicle for a moral. Let the tension build up to that major gaffe or close escape. You'll have your students' attention all the way.

Describing those experiences that are funny in hindsight can provide a model for students to laugh at themselves. "This happened to me, too," you are saying, "and it didn't kill me." Such stories can give perspective into challenging situations and communicate life lessons.

Well-told stories stick in our memories long after the telling is done. Funny stories, like songs, can help students remember facts and concepts. If creativity is what you love, go for it. Personify parts of the table of elements to show how they relate to each other. Describe the embarrassing scenario for which our intrepid hero will need math or science to escape. And history contains just as many "oopses" as our everyday life. Stories like that have a way of getting into us and staying there.

3. As an entry point to talk about stressors.

The better you know your students, their life situations, and their developmental stages, the better you can address the stressors they are experiencing. Stressors tend to cause us to feel the following: guilt, uncertainty, inadequacy, fear, sorry, hurt, isolation, embarrassment, and so on. Most people will sit and suffer before they bring up a subject that reveals such a hornet's nest of emotions. No one wants to look stupid.

If we can laugh about it, even a little, we can start the conversation.

Using humor in class allows teachers to point out some of the learning issues that are involved in common stressors. It allows us to broach such subjects as bad decisions, rebellion (and its consequences), misunderstandings, peer pressure, worries about appearance, challenges in relationships, and a host of developmental issues.

If we can laugh about it, we might not cry about it (or we might finally be able to cry about it, and get catharsis that way.) We realize that we are not alone, that we are not the only person on earth who has had such an experience. Humor helps us launch conversations in which we can name what is wrong; once an issue has a name, it can be addressed directly.

4. Revealing depth of understanding.

   Telling jokes and humorous stories necessitates the ability to discern a pattern within a situation and then to describe an unpredictable ending or new perspective. In terms of understanding, then, humor is much like the higher-order thinking skill of insight, discussed in Chapter 3. "Ha!" we say. "I'd never thought of it like that!"

   Consider inviting your students to use humor in their projects and presentations. Not only will they be more fun to watch and grade, but your students will be showing you, at a deep level, what they have learned.

Asking students to address a topic with a humorous perspective requires pattern recognition and plenty of creative thinking. In addition, they have to understand their audience. That requires knowing what stressors will engage their classmates and what alternative endings will relieve that stress in a funny way. It's complicated thinking. You might be surprised how creative and effective your students can be—not to mention how much fun they'll have doing the work.

When asking students to use humor as part of the presentations—when they choose to adapt the information into skits and videos and puppet shows, and so on—it is helpful to provide a rubric describing the content and audience issues you expect them to demonstrate.

Table 9.1

Rating	Humor
0	No attempt.
1	Humor did not illustrate a pattern that exists within the content • content ideas were not woven into a discernible pattern (goofy for no reason) • humor was isolated (like a joke) • audience stressors were inaccurate
2	The content pattern described was accurate • humor did not illuminate the content pattern • audience stressors were partially correct • alternative ending/new setting did not relieve audience stress
3	Humor and the content were addressed separately • content pattern was not connected to the audience • audience stressors were appropriate • alternative ending / new setting was appropriate
4	Humor was used to further define the content patterns and relationships • showed incongruities within the content and audience patterns • enhanced the understanding of the topic • integrated throughout the presentation • involves audience

Humor, like any skill, takes time and practice to develop. It takes modeling and clear expectations if you want it to be part of your students' grade. The nice thing about humor, though, is that most people already know how to be funny. They laugh and try to make others laugh in their normal, daily lives. You are simply inviting it into the classroom, recognizing when it helps students form a connection, recall information, or show (while having fun) just how much they've learned.

NOTES

1. Mowrer, R.R., S. S. Love, and D. B. Orem. "Desirable Teaching Qualities Transcend the Nature of the Student." *Teaching of Psychology* 31, no. 2. (2004): 775–790. The students were undergraduates, but the traits of effective teachers are relevant regardless of student age.

2. Mowrer, Love, and Orem, p. 107. The study compiled two "top ten" lists with remarkable agreement. The 7 items we've listed made both top ten lists. Not agreed-upon: one list included "confident" and "realistic expectations." The other listed "accessible" and "flexible." "Encouraging" (study 1) and "understanding" (study 2) have been combined into one in our list.

Chapter Ten

Being Explicit

What does it mean to be "on time?" Does "on time" for you mean showing up exactly on the dot, or five minutes before? Is a ten- or fifteen-minute window acceptable? Is whenever you get there good enough? If you assume that the person you are meeting has the same definition of "on time" that you do, one of you might end up waiting.

Five minutes here or there may not be a big deal. But we've all been in situations where our unspoken assumptions did not line up with another's. We used words we thought were clear, and the other person just didn't get it. Whether it's defining what a "clean house" means with your spouse, arranging a proper holiday with your in-laws, or assessing your students' learning, the more we can be explicit about what we want, the smoother everything is going to be.

Picture a sports team getting ready for the next big game. The players have gone through their drills and played a scrimmage, but the coach knows it just isn't enough. "You have to work harder," he tells his panting team. Maybe he shouts it; maybe he says it as part of a pep talk. It's apt advice. The problem is the players don't know what he means.

The coach might not know precisely what he means, either, until he sees it. Is he telling them to run faster, pass more often, or bring more energy or a better attitude to the game? The team has no idea. They can't read his mind. If he can't clarify his meaning, they'll just keep doing what they're doing, wondering if it's right.

IS THIS GOING TO BE ON THE TEST?

Story: When I first started having my students do science—act like scientists instead of learn a subject— they would frequently ask, "Is this going to be on the test?" It was a good question because I truly did not know how I was going to assess their overall learning.

I knew I wanted more than facts, but I myself was such a novice at doing science that I could not be explicit to myself or with my students about the overall learning expectations.

Over time, as I learned the skills, knowledge, and beliefs of acting like a scientist, I began to use rubrics that made my expectations for learning explicit. Skills were named and identified, connections emphasized, and thinking like a scientist modeled and valued.

The more explicit I made the learning expectations, the less frequently I heard the "on the test" question, and that was a good thing.

We have to be explicit about what we want our students to learn. We cannot assume that they will value the same information we do in reading through the textbook or listening in class.

Remember the anxiety that accompanied that first paper or exam in a new class? You clear your schedule to make the study session, hoping to find out what exactly is going to be on the test. Still, unless the teacher has been incredibly explicit about his or her expectations, you're left hoping you're on the right track, worrying you're focusing on the wrong thing. Remember how the second assignment, or the second course you took with that teacher, was easier? The subject could be hugely challenging, but at least you knew what he or she was looking for this time.

When we present key concepts in class, it's okay—it's necessary!—to label them as such. It's helpful to say, "Here is your take-home point for the day. This is a key idea that we'll keep running into throughout the semester." Sure, there's value in having students wade through information and sort out the key concepts. But in general, particularly in a short unit, do you want your students to spend their energy guessing what you think is important, or applying it?

If you value correct grammar as more important than ideas in a paper (or vice versa),

or if there are certain big names in the field that students need to be familiar with,

or if you simply want them to see the overall pattern,

or if committing a certain formula to memory will make the next month of class ten times easier, students need to know. Tell them directly what you are looking for, and tell them why you value that particular learning. Otherwise, simply too much work goes into guessing, and that's not where you want your students' time, effort, and resources to be spent.

Aligning your assessments to your learning expectations tells everyone where to spend their time, effort, and resources. Students are a function of their prior schooling experiences, and many believe that if it is not assessed, it is not important to learn.

If you want them to learn more than facts, then assess it—and tell them what it needs to look like. If you want them to learn new skills, then perfect practice is the norm. And if you want them to act like experts in your field, then have them practice thinking and valuing like an expert.

Most importantly of all, talk with them about what you expect, why it matters, and when they are done, what they have learned. Without the conversation, you are only hoping that they will guess what it is you wanted them to learn.

NAMING IS POWER

Story: When I was a senior in college I took a course on death and dying. Unsurprisingly, a lot of my friends were curious about my course choice. It wasn't directly in my major, and there weren't other clear reasons to assume that that subject would be one I'd pick up. I clarified, "Lots of people I know are going to die at some point. Assumedly everyone. Studying the way people respond to death sounds relevant and interesting to my life." That answer usually satisfied my friends' questions.

Six months later, my dad died suddenly. As I worked my way through the long grieving process, the theories and steps of grief I'd learned in class kept popping into my head. I found that when I was experiencing a certain emotion, I could label it according to all I'd learned, and that helped me not to feel like I was weird and alone.

Difficult though the experience was, I had confidence that what I was going through was okay. I knew that what I felt was part of a process, which meant that the way I felt at the moment wasn't how I was going to feel forever. Being able to name those emotions was incredibly liberating.

Whether you're talking about death or health, sex, marriage, or any other big topic, there's a tendency to think that we're the only ones who are struggling with questions. Left unasked, those questions fester and get harder to bring up. Maybe there's something seriously weird or wrong with us, we worry. Once we can talk explicitly about those questions, whatever they are, their power over us is diminished.

If you work with preteens or teenagers, puberty is on their minds. Without chances to talk about what they are experiencing, to name their feelings, the subject can overpower them. They could think about it every day, but they don't know the answers (and neither do their friends).

Being explicit takes the power away from those questions and puts the focus where you want it. It helps to say, "I suspect a lot of you are wondering about this. Let's name it and talk about it." Suddenly there's no longer an elephant in the room.

Is this chapter suggesting that you turn your classroom into a health class? Yes, according to the way it fits with your particular subject.

If you teach literature, choose some of the amazing literature that addresses coming of age. In the course of teaching students how to understand and analyze a text, they can find answers about themselves. They can talk about themselves safely in the context of literature.

If you teach history, well, there have been people their age in their exact situation throughout history. What did their lives look like? What did they struggle with? If you teach science, science is all about inquiry. You get the idea.

The more we can name our expectations and concerns—the more precise and articulate we can be—the better the dialogue we'll have. And that is a life lesson.

EXPLICIT WORLDVIEW

There's an expression: "The more you know, the less you know." In other words, the deeper you get into a new subject, the more you realize how much of it there is to learn. Those concepts that seemed so huge and difficult when we first learned them are only a shallow understanding compared to where we are now.

Story: After two years of high school French, I thought I could speak the language pretty well. I could order food and engage in small talk. My test scores confirmed my confidence. Then the French exchange students showed up for a week . . . and I realized that I hardly knew anything at all.

Once I realized how limited I actually was in my knowledge, I could change it. I now had a glimpse of just how much more there was to learn. Without that explicit understanding, I'd still be patting myself on the back for being able to order "un hamburger."

The same is true with any skill set we possess. As with knowledge, we don't know the limits of our skills until they are put to the test. Once you know where you stand, you can set up realistic learning goals to get yourself to where you want to go. Every time you realize you're not where you think you are, you have new opportunities for creativity, critical thinking, and learning.

Here's the hard part: the same is true for beliefs. While we might be quick to name our religion—beliefs with a capital *B*, if you will—there are myriad other beliefs—lowercase *b*—we've developed through life experience that we very rarely name or even recognize. We might hold beliefs about the abilities of our students, the safety of certain parts of town, the gender appropriateness of various tasks, and so on. The more we examine our beliefs, the more we understand how we see the world. We can make explicit the issues and beliefs that hold us prisoner to one way of thinking.

The real power of making beliefs explicit is when students become aware of what and how they think, of seeing life from new perspectives. We all have lenses that help us focus on what's important and block out extraneous information. But if we are unaware of those lenses or beliefs, we don't know what information we are missing. Our life experience and our beliefs shape our lens, as do our race, socioeconomic status, and sexual orientation. When we make those beliefs explicit, we are able to step back and see ourselves from others' perspectives, and that helps us relate to others.

Those factors affect how we teach. When we reflect on our beliefs and make them explicit, we can notice where we've made leaps of abstraction— places where we've assumed a pattern that might not actually exist. There's a temptation to say, "Generally, students respond this way every time I teach this lesson," or even, "Generally, the male basketball player who sits in the back of the room challenges me on these kinds of issues."

Stereotypes form this way. To combat them, we have to name our beliefs explicitly. Once they're in words, we can say, "Wait a minute, is that true? Based on how many examples?"

The more explicit our views of our knowledge, skills, and beliefs, the more effectively we can figure out where we are and where we want to go. Once we know where we stand, we can keep or change what we want to. We can set up realistic learning goals for ourselves and others. Our classes run just a little more smoothly, as long as we keep evaluating where we are.

Chapter Eleven

Real and True

Making It Mean Something for Students

There is a *Calvin and Hobbes* comic strip where Calvin's teacher is complaining about all the stuff Calvin does not know: dates, math facts, and so on. In the next frame Calvin turns the inquisition around, asking Ms. Wormwood about all the stuff he cares about that she doesn't know. Calvin's comments point out an important concept: only the facts you value are important.

We are products of our genetics and our experiences (and the interactions between the two). We choose what to learn. What we choose to learn at a given time and place is what best meets our interests and needs (or so we believe).

We know that, regardless of their performance in the classroom, people are capable of learning all sorts of things to meet their needs. The student who daydreams through math might be able to recite every important baseball statistic from the last five decades. The student who rolls her eyes through grammar can communicate just fine to friends via three or four different kinds of technology.

We cannot make anyone learn anything unless they choose to. The best we can do is to put them into situations where the hoped-for learning will meet their needs. This could be as simple as reminding Johnny that if he wants to be a doctor, as he says, then he'll need to master chemistry. Alternatively, it could involve reenvisioning some of your lesson plans.

When approaching new material, learners will generally have two questions. They are questions you asked yourself when you first picked up the book, and the answers determine which chapters you'll skim or skip, and which you'll decide to read:

1. Is it relevant? *Merriam-Webster* defines *relevant* as "having significant and demonstrable bearing on the matter at hand." In other words, does it satisfy your needs?
2. Is it meaningful? In other words, is there a "meaning" or a "purpose" for you to learn this? (*Merriam-Webster* again.)

Good teachers do their best to make their classes meaningful and relevant to their students. The motivations we may throw out to them, however, are sometimes too far beyond their scope of understanding to be effective. To make learning Real and True means focusing on making learning relevant and meaningful to the student(s) right now, today, this minute in time.

Real means that the learning that the teacher is asking the students to complete falls within their *timeframe of caring*. Telling students that they'll need to know something when they grow up, go to college, get married, or have a job generally will not provide enough motivation to change their behavior today. Important though those things are, they are simply too far off into the future to feel Real to students; they are beyond their timeframe of caring.

True means that there is a high probability that it will actually happen in the future. True ultimately is viewed as a trust issue for many students. Do they trust the teacher enough to believe their predictions about the future? Is their teacher reliable and believable enough that the learning task becomes worth their time, effort, and resources to learn the material today?

Learning that is both Real and True is seen by students as being both relevant and meaningful—and that allows them to give of their time, effort, and resources.

MOVING AT THE SPEED OF TECHNOLOGY

Consider all the activities calling upon kids' attention. There are sports and other organizations at school. There are friends, Facebook, and other addictive bits of technology. What you're asking your students to do for your class has to be more important than all of the other things they find massively interesting.

What's more, technology is changing the world at an ever-quicker pace, to the extent that they might not need to know once-important information in college. Computers have drastically changed the way we do research and present information. In a world where we can look up information quickly and easily on any number of portable devices, the threat that "you'll need to have this memorized for later" holds little water.

The more quickly the world changes, the harder it's going to be to be to make those True predictions about when and how students will need what they learn in the classroom. If you can't connect it directly to their lives today yet are still asking them to do it, you're moving from a learning issue to a trust issue. "Trust me," you tell your students. "This will matter later. You will need to know it."

You might be able to get away with statements like these once or twice, but unless you're making investments into your students' emotional bank accounts (getting to know them and leading them into meaningful learning in other areas), that emotional bank account is going to run dry before the school year ends.

This change in required learning has been in motion for decades. When cars were new on the roads, potential owners had to prove they could fix a car before they could buy it. Happily, we don't have to be mechanics any more to drive cars. The process is just too complicated. Just because the role of mechanic has been taken off our plates doesn't mean we have become lazy or less motivated; it just allows us to focus on other subjects. There is no shortage of things to learn.

Technology changes, but helping students learn how to think never goes out of style. Students can access information more quickly than ever before, but the challenge is knowing what to do with that information. Those creative and critical thinking skills may be more important than ever before.

Take anatomy and physiology, for example. Imagine the students' complaints when they are told they have to memorize all 206 bones in the body, when they know they can simply look up the answer if needed. You could remind them that we can't think without facts, that they need to know these names and functions in order to understand how the body works. You could dangle a heavily weighted test over their heads and let fear of bad grades be the motivator.

Instead, you turn the assignment into one that is application-based. Imagine telling students, "Design a bone that can do these three tasks." The tasks are such that students will have to look at all the different kinds of bones and figure out how they work. Now they are learning and applying what they know rather than simply learning names. Over the course of the project, they will absorb the facts they need. They will even memorize the bones they reference most often in order to save the time of looking them up.

Having access to the Internet is like taking an open-book test. At first pass it might sound easier, but in fact this format is testing learning at a higher level. The questions the students face require them to *do something* with their information. They have to know how to recognize and use their tools. Those skills remain relevant no matter how technology changes.

A learning task must meet the needs of the learner. That statement sounds redundant and obvious until you consider the plethora of audiences learning tasks are normally designed to satisfy: teachers, parents, district-wide content groups, administration, assessment committees, school boards, and state and national agencies.

For any learning task to be Real and True, it must meet the needs of the learner first. If the learning task meets the needs of any other audience, then so much the better. Certainly an excellent lesson could please many of these other audiences. But what matters in learning, ultimately, is the individual or group who is going to learn from the task and be changed by it.

PRIORITIES

Here's a common question with, as usual, a big answer: "What's your job?" Below are four possible answers.

- I'm a content expert.
- I'm a [subject] teacher.
- I'm a teacher of [subject].
- I'm a teacher of people.

There is no right or wrong answer to this question. Rather, the way you define your job shows how you prioritize what you do. Your answer defines what is "real and true" to you as the teacher.

If you see yourself as a science teacher, then what you're trying to do is get your students to build up a warehouse of science facts and understanding. If you teach people, then you have a different way of prioritizing what it is that you teach.

When you teach people of any age, in any subject, it's important to know your students as individuals within a developmental and cultural context. All that first-day-of-school, getting-to-know-you stuff matters: their hobbies and interests, their sports and clubs, what they read, listen to, and watch. This stuff matters because it gives you a glimpse into what is meeting their needs. You can get a sense of their concerns and stressors, their experiences and releases. It helps you know how your students view the world.

You can actually measure how meaningful a task is to someone else by considering three basic questions. How much time do they put into the task? How concentrated is their focus? How many resources of their own did they contribute?

Asking these questions about a person's hobby, for example, is a good way to determine how meaningful that hobby is. Say, in the course of getting to know a neighbor, you learn that she is into biking. You often see her on her bike, and she's put in some significant miles. You see her putting air in the tires, wiping off mud, working on the chain—clearly she is focused on her task. She owns a nice bike and bike gear, which means she has invested her resources in this hobby. After such a study of her behaviors, you could conclude that biking is a meaningful hobby for your neighbor. Her actions speak for themselves.

People expect to spend time, energy, and resources on the things that are relevant to them. The question is, how are your students spending their time? Spending hours on Facebook or online gaming, for example, may seem like a waste to some, but those activities indicate what is meaningful to them: connecting with others, staying in the loop, and having fun.

What you're asking students to learn has to connect to their lives outside the school setting. They have to see it as meeting their needs and being worthy of their time. It is, after all, a competition. There are only twenty-four hours in a day.

When we talk about motivation for learning, teachers (as adults) like intrinsic reasons. Most of us who choose to spend our lives in education settings think learning is motivating for learning's sake—an intrinsic reason. Lifelong learners choose to learn because doing so meets their needs.

These motivations are important to talk about, but most kids aren't at that point yet developmentally. Still, they might have other intrinsic reasons for wanting to learn, such as finding a subject interesting. "I like to read" or "I like to make things with my hands" are statements of intrinsic motivation.

Grades, by contrast, are extrinsic motivators. They can be highly effective for some students. It is okay to talk about grades in class, or the idea that school is a kid's "job," as long as these aren't presented as the only possible motivators for success.

> *Story: One of my students recently explained to me her motivation in choosing high school science courses. She had to take either physics or chemistry; the school did not require her to take both, nor did she have room in her schedule. Both classes, she thought, sounded equally difficult. She chose physics because, as she explained, it dealt with things she could see. For that reason, she thought it might prove more relevant to her life than chemistry.*

Ideally, our students will have both intrinsic and extrinsic motivations in our classes. In the case of this student, she was intrinsically motivated by the hope of learning useful knowledge. She was extrinsically motivated to complete her high school science requirement. Those were her realities and expectations walking into physics on that first day. If she had to take the course, she wanted it to matter in her life.

TAPPING INTO WHAT'S REAL AND TRUE

Letting students pick the format and topic of their final projects can be entry points into meaningful work, as it allows students to invest time into what they find relevant in a particular unit. But deeper than that, every subject is based on big ideas that matter here and now. Any field of study, at its root, can be relevant to any student—no matter what life experiences, genetic predispositions, or technological influences they have in their lives.

The purpose of literature, for example, is to give expression to the human experience, into what life is and can be. Given the range of classical works, you can choose literature with themes your students may have lived through or thought about, thus giving them a platform for investigation.

William Shakespeare remains classic because his story lines are relevant in each generation. *Romeo and Juliet* is a play about teenage love and the urgent feelings that others around the protagonists just don't understand. As students debate whether their three-day love affair really was love, they are talking about experiences that are relevant and meaningful to their own lives—while practicing literary analysis.

As for history, you can't open a history book without finding an example of someone facing an obstacle or living through an experience that is every bit as engaging as our best literature. We have all seen the texts that act as though only white male generals and politicians were alive in a given time period; to look only at those figures is to give up a powerful entry point of discussion for students.

Every single person in those history books was once the same age as the students in your classroom. Exploring the lives and values of people your students' age in a given time period can bring history alive and connect today's students to the past.

Mathematics invites us to look for and describe patterns in the world in order to make predictions. Science invites us to notice and solve problems in an attempt to understand the world around us. The problem-solving tools used in both fields are empowering to students both inside and outside of the classroom.

Every content area has a purpose, and that purpose connects with students' lives here and now. It's just a matter of communicating that purpose to students, and for that we turn to the next chapter.

Chapter Twelve

Where Are We Going,
and Why Does It Matter?

Have you ever sat on a committee where you've had to come up with a mission statement? The talk can drag on for hours, ranging from such big questions as "Who are we?" and "What is our goal?" down to endless rounds of hairsplitting debates over wording.

It's a high-stakes game, getting an entire committee to agree on one common vision and purpose for existence. That mission statement has to sum up what you believe and where you're going. It's a difficult conversation.

Outside of planning meetings and religious discussions, we rarely talk about purpose. It's such a grand term and a personal one. Words like "vision" and "purpose" get thrown around interchangeably, further complicating the issue. Let's start with definitions, which are adapted from Peter Senge's book, *The Fifth Discipline*.

Your *purpose* is a big, abstract, overarching idea that spans a lifetime. It answers the question, "Why do you do what you do?" Our purpose explains how we allocate our time and energy. Your purpose might be to be a good parent, an active member of your community, an advocate for students in trouble, and so on. Most adults have more than one purpose.

Rick Warren's best-selling books from the early 2000s, *The Purpose Driven Life* and *The Purpose Driven Church,* are excellent examples of the lifelong, deep-reaching scope of a purpose. The high sales demonstrate how hungry many people are to have that conversation.

Having a purpose allows you to set *visions* for yourself. Visions are concrete actions that align with your purpose. If your purpose is to be a lifelong learner, your visions might include graduating from college or learning to play a new instrument well enough to perform in front of others. Both of these are clear goals, and you'll know when you've achieved them.

Let's say that one of your purposes for yourself is to live a healthy lifestyle. For years, the vision that has fit with this purpose has been to swim regularly. Then one year, you get a new job in a town where you no longer have pool access. Do you give up on a healthy lifestyle?

No (hopefully)! Your purpose remains the same; you simply need to find a new vision to meet those needs. You peruse your options, and perhaps you join a basketball team instead. Or find a walking partner. The point is, you can still live up to your purpose.

Likewise, how you live a healthy lifestyle will continue to change as you age. Because your purpose is broader than any one sport or location, you continue to be able to set new, measurable visions to keep fulfilling that purpose.

There are three key components to setting and meeting a purpose. The first is to remember what your purpose is. If you don't know why you're doing something, you get frustrated and lose focus. You can call upon your purpose of living a healthy lifestyle on those days when a workout feels like too much effort and those "golden arches" look like a convenient dinner option.

The second key is to start small. You need to have enough successes to keep you going. If you have a vision to run a marathon, but you've never done more than two miles, you're going to be in enormous trouble unless you work your way up to your goal.

You have to equip yourself with proper running shoes and the right diet. You have to be on a training program that allows you to build gradually and celebrate your successes. Otherwise, you'll give up.

Small successes are like checkpoints along a race. They let us know we're making progress, and they give us manageably sized challenges to face one at a time. Those successes along the way are like the scaffolding on a building project, allowing us to climb higher next time without getting too overwhelmed.

This scaffolding strategy rings true whether you are getting in shape or designing a new classroom learning task or learning environment. Take it step by step, with a purpose.

The third key is to have others alongside of you who support you in your learning and provide that precious love and belonging that Dr. William Glasser has identified as one of our basic needs (see Chapter 2). We need the support of others—emotionally, intellectually, and morally—depending on the need at that moment in time.

Story: When I was heavy into home remodeling, I would usually attempt to fix the problem on my own. Then, when I got in over my head, I'd stop over at my neighbor's. He was one of those guys who knew everything about home repair, and he was always willing to take twenty minutes to show me how things worked.

I didn't want to know the whole thing right away—just the next step. He'd show me, then I'd go practice. He didn't mind that, a few days later, I'd be back with a new question.

That friendly, practical support helped me achieve my visions by completing repair job after repair job, aligning with my purposes of being a lifelong learner and understanding how things work.

In our classrooms, we teachers are part of that support network that helps students achieve their visions.

VISION QUESTS

When you were an undergraduate education major, you were on a vision quest. Your vision quest was to graduate with a teaching certificate and, following that, to get a job as a teacher.

You had a clear and measurable vision, and it required a lot of hard work to achieve. Focusing on your vision helped you to make some tough decisions. Were you going to do homework or watch TV? Prepare tomorrow morning's lesson or go out with friends? Motivation to do well comes from wanting the vision more than other choices you could make.

Vision quests are *meant* to be hard. They are journeys that require hours—years—of preparation and toil, and they don't always come with clear maps that show the road ahead. If it's not hard, we as humans frequently don't see it as valuable. Failure is part of what makes success so sweet. Despair shows us our inner strength. The journey itself is important.

All through an education major's college career, it might feel like enough just to have that vision of becoming a teacher. But what happens once you land that teaching job? Once you've been teaching for a year or two, then what? What's next? Maybe you'll choose to enter a master's program, at which point you'll have another clear vision: to get that degree. But then what?

Once you've achieved that vision, you need a new one, and in order to do that, you need to connect to the larger purpose that made teaching so desirable in the first place. Is it to make a difference in the lives of children? To use teaching as a form of social activism? To maintain a comfortable work-life balance?

Without that clear purpose, whatever it is, we begin to lose focus and burn out. With a clear purpose, we can set the next vision—the next small step for where we want to go. By keeping our eyes focused on that purpose, particularly when the journey is winding and unclear, we can remember why we are doing what we do.

THE PURPOSE-DRIVEN CLASSROOM

The good news is, you don't have to wait until your students are in college to talk about purpose. Purpose, after all, is intrinsically tied with our motivation. It's hard to marshal motivation when you don't know what you want. And getting that next degree, while motivating to some, is not a purpose— it's a vision that helps us get there.

We talked in the previous chapter about connecting the work of the classroom with what is meaningful to students in their present moment. If you know a student wants to be a doctor or a sports announcer or a car mechanic, tying your classroom instruction into that interest can be a powerful motivator. But what about the learners (young and old) who don't know what they want to be when they grow up?

You don't have to have a career plan in mind in order to have a purpose. Many students don't know what they want to be when they grow up, and even if they do, there's a good chance it might change.

Most students, however, do have a sense of the *kind* of person they want to be. They may want to be loyal friends, honest citizens, or supportive members of their family. They may want to embody certain values they see in their parents—or they may want to be the exact opposite of what they see at home.

When it comes to helping a student find his or her purpose, the question isn't, "What do you want to be?" It's, "What do you want to be *like?*" What attributes do you want to embody? The answer to that question is hugely important to students.

Let's talk about that in the classroom. The critical thinking, decision-making, idea-articulating skills they are learning in your classroom can connect deeply to your students' lives when they consider the kind of person they want to become.

Put it another way. In general, people don't mean to screw up their lives. They are, in general, doing the best they can. Our job is to help them make better choices with an end in mind, which means they need to know what that end is. When we talk with our students about purpose, we are able to say, "You are where you are, and that's okay. Where are you going?" If they have a purpose to be a certain kind of person, then they will be able to learn and set visions and make choices in ways that are real and true to them.

How well does all this identity-forming, motivation-building work align with our actual subject material? Very well, if you think in terms of the big picture.

Take science, for example. The overall purpose of science is problem noticing and problem solving. Most of the great scientific discoveries throughout history came because someone noticed a problem and attempted to solve it. That kind of work is highly relevant to kids, both now and for their futures.

As it is, they have no other mechanism to notice and solve problems. They might attribute outcomes to luck, circumstance, or hard work. If you ask a student to go through and explain how she noticed a problem and came up with a solution, chances are, she won't be able to articulate it—until she learns how to do so.

In a class that focuses on memorizing information, students have no way to see the larger purpose. At each unit, they have to start again at zero, and the previous unit is at risk of being packed up and forgotten. But once we see science in the light of its purpose—to notice and solve problems—it allows our students to approach physics, biology, earth science, and chemistry in a new and meaningful way. Now the ideas build upon each other from unit to unit and year to year. The problems and techniques change, but the problem-solving approach and sense of discovery remain.

In approaching science this way, students learn far more than the course material. They are also coming to see how they can be in control of their decisions. Suddenly, what happens in science matters outside of the classroom as well as inside. There's a purpose to science, far beyond learning the material or passing the class. The same goes for all other subjects.

Learning is fun and exciting. It's interesting and engaging, and it's infinitely worth our time, effort, and resources when it connects to our larger purpose.

Chapter Thirteen

Inquiry

The Process That Continues to Give

Everyone expects the teacher to know the answer—especially the teacher. After all, we're the ones with the degrees. We're the ones who designed the lesson, who determined which material to cover and how to approach it. If a student asks a question we can't answer, it's easy to feel frustrated, flat-footed, ill-prepared. Isn't knowing the answer our job?

And so, we set up our classrooms, as much as possible, so that students can come to us for the final word on the subject. We teach our content, we explain how things work, and they, in turn, come to trust our ability and authority. That's what we're supposed to do, right?

Setting up a lesson where we might not know the answers would undermine our authority, wouldn't it?

That depends on how you go about the process of inquiry.

Inquiry is a life skill. There are no jobs where math people open up a math textbook and do problems. There are no jobs where scientists sit in rooms by themselves exclusively memorizing formulas.

Instead, most jobs for which college students train require people to use the skills they have learned in order to do problem solving and inquiry. In a rapidly changing world, the ability to identify a problem and find a new solution may be the most important skill a worker can bring. The more inquiry can be modeled in the classroom, the more prepared students will be for untold demands later on.

And yet, in a future-focused classroom—one that teaches students to inquire and solve problems in a given discipline—the correct answer can't always be forthcoming. In addition to teaching our content, we are teaching our students to enter the unknown. They—and we—have to get comfortable with not knowing all the answers right away. They—and we—have to start seeing "I don't know" as an opportunity for learning rather than as a sign of failure.

Inquiry is a process, with specific steps that each require a different pattern of thinking. Educator Donald Schön argues that there are seven steps of inquiry that fit with any discipline. His seven steps, slightly adjusted, are as follows:

1. Observations
2. Being curious
3. Problem statements
4. Gathering information
5. Action steps*
6. Analysis of data
7. Conclusion

Each step requires a different set of skills. While the steps are iterative, always pointing you back to the question at hand, you have to think differently at different times. When you're gathering information online, that's a different set of skills than choosing a problem to focus on or deciding what the data tells you. One step is not more important than another, but you have to think in different ways to accomplish different tasks.

Notice that "stating the problem" does not come until the third step. There are times—in life, work, and classroom exercises—when we are handed a problem and must go from there.

Problem: my computer stopped working.

Problem: solve this proof.

Problem: the allies after World War I must devise a fair treaty to end the Great War and bring about peace. Here's the problem; now do something to solve it.

If we want our students to develop the lifelong skill of inquiry, however, we have to teach all seven of these steps. We have to be explicit about what we are doing. Which brings us back to steps one and two: observation and being curious.

Beyond about third grade, most students don't come to class curious because they are accustomed to the teacher controlling the learning environment and providing the answers. The problems are always provided for them.

If we want students to be curious, we have to teach them how to do so. Give students the tools of your discipline: the pulleys and levers, the great debates, the clay or paint or charcoal, and let them play. Let them be curious, and tell them why you're doing it.

Story: In teaching high school, I used to require my students to write "I wonder" statements. And because I wanted them to think creatively, I assigned them to come up with fifty or seventy-five such statements. The first time I did it, they were furious. They were being asked to think in a new way, a way that had not been necessary in their previous science classes. Some students thought I was wasting their time.

By the end of the year, however, they got good at wondering. I had students coming into my class and asking, "Did you ever wonder about . . . ?" My students, like all great thinkers and inventors, were learning to notice problems, and their curiosity led us to a number of teachable moments.

Once the problem has been clearly established, the next steps on the list will seem logical and familiar. We must find the resources around us and arm ourselves with relevant information.

Students in this stage often mistake gathering information with copying. They are excellent at locating and copying data, but that does not necessarily mean they will take the time to engage with the information and understand what they've written down. Consider making it a rule that students can get credit for gathering information only if they can answer your questions about what their information means.

The fifth step, "action steps," has an asterisk by it because it varies by discipline. Each discipline has a different set of tools and expectations a person must follow between researching a problem and being able to analyze data. Conducting a scientific experiment would fall in this category.

Only after all these steps have been completed can we analyze our data and draw conclusions. Again, the specific subject will dictate the exact form that our analysis and conclusions take.

In the course of reaching their final conclusions, students are engaged in creative thinking, critical thinking, and problem solving. That's the commonality of doing inquiry in any field of study. Being observant and curious requires creative thinking. Defining the problem, choosing the action steps, and choosing criteria by which to analyze the data involve critical thinking. Inquiry is creative thinking, critical thinking, and problem solving wrapped together in a messy world.

Let's look at two examples of what inquiry in the class might look like.

1. Physical education

Imagine you are a physical education (PE) teacher and you want to teach a unit on rules (which addresses the purpose of physical education/health—decision-making). Thinking about having your students *do* inquiry, you begin by explaining the big picture of the unit (rules and how rules apply to decision-making). Then you have them play three games: baseball, soccer, and tennis (any three different games would work). Then you ask them,

"What is it about the rules of the game that makes you curious?" You have then come up with numerous "I wonder" statements dealing with the rules of the game.

They then take their most interesting "I wonder" statement and turn it into a problem statement that provides a specific direction for their project. The problem could be measuring the impact of a rule change in a game.

So now it's time for some research into their problem statement. They read, interview, and Google rule changes. Finally, they design an action plan that involves playing a game, changing the rules, and measuring the impact of that rule change. They collect some data, find out what it means, and then communicate how changing the rules of a game impacts the nature of the game itself.

Doing inquiry allows them to understand that whatever rules are in place have a direct impact upon the nature of the game. It also allows them to experience the fact that rules are man-made: people made them, and people can change them. If the rule no longer works, change the rules. This is powerful learning (while still being physically active during PE time).

2. Social Studies

Imagine you are a social studies teacher and you want to teach a unit on perseverance (which addresses the purpose of social studies—understanding the human experience). Thinking about having your students *do* inquiry, you begin by explaining the big picture of the unit (perseverance and how staying committed to a powerful idea is part of the human experience).

Then you have them experience three cases of people who have perse-vered; maybe a guest speaker, a DVD interview, and a reading (any three powerful examples would work—the closer the person is to their age, the better). Then you ask them, "What is it about perseverance that makes you curious?" You have then come up with numerous "I wonder" statements dealing with the stick-to-itiveness.

They then take their most interesting "I wonder" statement and turn it into a problem statement that provides a specific direction for their project. The problem could be clarifying the human characteristics that allow someone to persevere in the face of overwhelming odds.

So now it's time for some research into their problem statement. They read, interview, and Google people who have persevered. Finally, they de-sign an action plan that might involve interviewing a specific person who has persevered, doing primary research into someone from history who is known to have persevered, or perhaps conducting a survey among their peers about qualities that impact perseverance. They collect some data, find out what it means, and then communicate what they have discovered about perseverance and the human experience.

Doing inquiry allows them to understand that perseverance is a human quality, not just something that famous people have. It also allows them to find out for themselves which perseverance qualities they already have and which they might choose to strengthen. This is powerful learning (while still being engaged in social studies learning).

But, you might ask, can't that inquiry process sidetrack the class away from learning important content? What happens when they ask questions I don't know the answer to?

That's where the fun begins.

BACKDOOR LEARNING

There is a fear that if you teach inquiry-focused learning, you won't be able to cover course content. The reality is that you and your students will cover huge amounts of content, although not always in the order you expected.

> *Story: I once had a group of students who decided that in order to complete the assigned experiment, they needed a piece of glass shaped like an S. Their proposed approach was creative and reasonable, but I didn't have glass rods shaped the way they wanted.*
>
> *So I gave them straight glass rods instead. Together we got out old science manuals, and they literally spent three days learning how to bend glass so they could do their project. My students chose to take on quite a bit of extra learning, and because they were self-motivated, they will remember the results.*

What that group of students experienced is called backdoor learning. The project looked easy enough at the start, but as they got more invested, they realized all the things they needed to know in order to get the task done (kind of like life). They accrued extra knowledge along the way, knowledge they would not have been nearly so motivated to gain if it had been assigned directly.

Let's apply this to a different field. The point of music theory is to understand and create beautiful music. In order to get there, you have to understand a complex series of rules about the way music works. The process of inquiry invites you turn the traditional order—individual rules carefully learned and strictly applied until the person is ready to create beautiful music—on its head.

The process of inquiry would, say, give students Finale or similar music-composing software. Let them play and compose. Let them express themselves and get frustrated and even hit a brick wall when they don't know what comes next. Then offer them music theory, piece by piece, as the occasion arises.

Suddenly the rule of thirds looks like a fabulous, useful shortcut rather than a rule to memorize and identify on a listening test. Hitting a brick wall helped them realize how much they need to know. Music theory becomes a dynamic tool with a product they can be proud of.

The inquiry process can be invigorating for you as a teacher. You get to watch students discover, and changing up the order of learning can keep the subject material fresh for you.

If, however, your learning style means that you are reading this, thinking, "It's all out of order. That sounds like too much work and chaos," don't worry. Just because there is space in the class for students to come up with their own questions and pursue learning-worthy side concepts does not mean that the class is disorganized. You are still the one in the room who is master of the content, and you know best when and how to present students with the pieces that they need.

The difference is that, because of the teachable moments you have engineered, students realize they need the information before you offer it to them. When you can jump on those teachable moments, suddenly learning seems relevant. And chances are, because they are taking a backdoor approach, they will likely learn (and remember) far more information than you could otherwise address.

PROCESS VS. PRODUCT: A MIS-FRAMED DEBATE

The resistance to inquiry-based learning seems to lie in an either-or assumption. There is an idea that you can either have process or product. Students can either learn how to get at the answer, or they can learn the required content.

The truth is that it's not an *either-or* situation; it's an *and* situation. Both are possible. Inquiry says that you can have process and learn content, because the answer to the process is in the content. The dilemma is that students in an inquiry-focused course may not learn a specific fifty facts. They may learn one hundred facts that partially overlap with the original list.

The facts that they learn will be organized differently. They won't be organized according to a chapter in a book; they'll be organized for each learner's brain. The end result is that students will learn (and remember) more content, and that learning is more likely to stick.

Granted, it'll be hard to give a test. Projects may be far more useful assessment tools for an inquiry-based class.

Teaching inquiry allows you to take the long view when it comes to content. You no longer have to make sure students learn everything in one particular learning sequence. Rather, the class approaches information in a spiral pattern. You never really leave the key concepts of the course; you simply return to them over and over with more knowledge. What a student does not grasp the first time around may become clear on the second or third spiral. There are always more sequences to come.

Another advantage of teaching inquiry is that its very nature requires you to understand context. All the facts we have are also determined by place and time. What was once revolutionary—the idea that the earth went around the sun, the speed of light, the concept of love between social classes—is now part of the culture.

When we simply learn the facts and concepts, we miss the fact that this knowledge once changed the face of the world. We miss the mystery and the wonder of discovery. The more we place ourselves within the context of the original inquiry, the more we understand about how the world works and changes.

An atom can be an item on a chart with parts to memorize, or it can be an electrifying, controversial concept, if imagined within the context of its original discovery. What made Albert Einstein great was not that he had all the answers but that he put out a coherent idea that drove inquiry for the next fifty years. As students see the processes of inquiry in the past, they can come to understand the inquiry going on around them now.

DIVERSE STUDENTS, DIVERSE DISCIPLINES

Inquiry is a naturally differentiated learning process. You as a teacher are saying, "Here's the topic, but I expect each of you to come up with your own question and sequence to address it." You set the definitive limits as to tools, process, time frame, and assessment expectations. Within those boundaries, though, students have wide choices and plenty of ownership.

Regardless of their experiences, skills, and thinking patterns, students can all find a way of addressing their topic and reaching a solution. Inquiry, for example, allows students to choose their own books, within guidelines, that address a class theme. However you approach it, the process allows them to find relevance in the topic you are studying.

For some teachers, the subject of student choice will send them page flipping back to Chapter 4 and its discussion of power in the classroom. For each activity, for each specific class, we end up asking a series of questions:

How much power must I keep? What can I share? What choices can I give students? How much will I allow them to risk? How much will I risk, myself?

There is no hard-and-fast answer to these questions; the answers shift with the circumstances. A tidy little adage for making these decisions is, "Keep what you must. Share what you can. Give what you dare." If you do inquiry in your classroom and can prove your students are learning, you can give them a fair amount of power.

You've switched from being the grand purveyor of all answers to a guide in the inquiry process. The safety nets are set up to ensure success.

Science, math, fine arts, history, all the content areas: inquiry works with any discipline. That said, not every question is appropriate for every field. Each field is designed to ask certain types of questions, and each field answers questions in its own way. When we try to use the wrong process for a question, or when we ask a question the field is not designed to answer, that's where problems come in.

For example, take the question "Where did life begin?" That question looks different when it is posed in religious, philosophical, and scientific settings. When people asking a religious question try to use science to find the answer, the result tends to be a messy discussion. The fault is not with the process of inquiry; the fault is with where the question is applied.

That's why a liberal arts view is helpful in the process of inquiry, because no matter what questions you have, they will fall within some classical liberal arts study. The more inquiry students do in different fields, the more quickly they recognize how these questions work.

In-depth inquiry takes time, but for the right questions, the results are rewarding. Some questions in life can be solved with simple decision-making. What to have for dinner, to pick a mundane example, does not require inquiry. But the big questions do. Finding a new home or vehicle or career, learning the way the world works, discovering why historical decisions were made: these challenges are worth the time, effort, and resources required for conducting an in-depth inquiry.

And the results of that learning will remain with us for a long time.

Chapter Fourteen

Flexible yet Focused

Teacher Flexibility

The introduction of this book mentioned a favorite "pearls of wisdom" exercise, in which educators working on their master's degrees would have to describe the top three ideas (pearls) that contributed to their success as teachers. It was a fun activity that generated good classroom discussion, but what was most surprising was the consistency of the results.

Every time, the first or second pearl on each instructor's list was teacher flexibility. The teachers told story after classroom story about how taking a flexible approach to reaching learning goals allowed their students to learn and surprise them along the way. Teacher flexibility ranked more important than organization or humor, the other top finishers.

In a diverse classroom, in times of change, it's no surprise that flexibility might be the most important trait to support a hardworking teacher. Every student is unique, and it's helpful when our approach to learning shows that. Before getting into what teacher flexibility is, let's pause a moment to consider what it isn't.

CHAOS THEORY

There is a difference between chaos and open-endedness.

Chaos is a classroom with no structure and no clear direction. The teacher might have a hope or wish for where the lesson will go, but it is not communicated to the students. There are no checkpoints for students and teacher alike to make sure that everyone is on the right track, and although there might be a purpose to the classroom, there is no clear, attainable vision. We are not advocating for chaos.

What effective teacher flexibility leads to, on the other hand, is an open-ended approach to the classroom. The structure of the class is clear to all who are involved, but it is flexible enough to allow for alternative pathways. Students are able to make choices within a tightly defined structure. The vision is always clear, but the path to reach it can be determined by each student.

The key difference between chaos and open-endedness is knowing where you are going—and communicating that plan explicitly to your students. Everything you do, every student choice you allow, is done with the end in mind. You know what learning you expect to happen, what understanding you hope your students will reach. The path is negotiable, but the check-points are firm requirements.

Every student can choose his or her own topic for an essay, for example, but all students have to hand in their notes, make some kind of outline or map, use a certain number of sources, and meet specific requirements for writing style, format, and length. If students are meeting all those steps, honing their research and writing skills, what does it matter which topic they choose to get there? (Plus, more variety makes for more interesting grading.)

Why is an open-ended approach necessary? Whether the populations of our classrooms are shifting, or we are simply acknowledging this reality more than we used to, classes are becoming more diverse. These range of diversities are extensive:

Table 14.1

Socioeconomic	Gender	Cultural
Developmental	Racial	Religious
Readers/nonreaders	Multiple intelligences	Learning styles
Gender/sexuality issues	EL/ESL	and more!

Though they may offer valuable learning opportunities, these lists of student diversity can get overwhelming in a hurry. Sometimes all the additional things we're supposed to consider in a diverse classroom can leave us feeling like we're taking a hammer and chisel to our lesson plans, trying to fit in everything we need while still maintaining organization and control.

Scores of books and teacher in-service days all offer advice on how to "address" this "issue," as though the ideal classroom were a homogenous one. Diversity requires more teacher flexibility, yes, but it also provides extensive opportunities for learning.

If the goal is to get from A to Z, there are many ways other than taking one straight line to get there. These alternative paths add interest for everyone involved, and they add opportunities for students to shine by contributing their unique talents and experiences to the classroom.

> *Story: I once had a boy named Ray whom I could not get to talk in class. It was clear from his body language that he had things to contribute, but I simply could not get him to open his mouth.*
>
> *At one point during the school year, I gave the students an option of rapping about their learning instead of giving a traditional report. Ray chose to rap, and he was fantastic. Our entire class never viewed him the same after that day—and afterward I could hardly get him to be quiet!*

Incidents like this, which allow students to demonstrate their learning in an alternative way and shine, add a sense of involvement in the classroom that was not there before. Students see what their peers have to offer, and new learning opportunities are born.

We said before that teacher flexibility was not an invitation to chaos. It is also *not* a lowering of expectations. The ways students meet our expectations can change. The means can vary, but the end—our explicit learning objectives, assignment criteria, and grading rubrics—do not waver.

KNOW THY STUDENTS

It takes some work to be flexible in the classroom, and it requires a shift in thinking, but the results are absolutely worthwhile. Teacher flexibility requires that teachers:

- Know students developmentally and maintain developmentally appropriate expectations.
- Know students as individuals with academic strengths and weaknesses; as with effective coaching, learners do well when they can maintain what they are good at while focusing specifically on what needs to be improved.
- Accept students where they are and work to move them to the next step, rather than focusing on where we wish or expect them to be.
- Possess the belief that *using* information to complete a task—as opposed to learning it by rote—puts more facts into their long-term memories.
- Know content well enough to understand what the big ideas are that hold the field together; this helps us keep an eye on what's worth learning as well as how the field creates new information.
- Believe that fun, appropriately challenging work is part of the learning journey.

- Believe that treating a class as a team has powerful, positive learning outcomes (more on this in a moment).

With these powerful foundations in place, we as teachers can confidently give students the choice as to how they will demonstrate their learning.

Consider students who have trouble reading. Unless the assignment is a reading task, the way they get their information is open-ended, and therefore a teacher flexibility issue. Could they conduct interviews instead? Could they view DVDs or listen to audio books? They will still have assignments that work on improving their reading skills. If a particular assignment allows them to gather information and demonstrate their learning in other ways, students may have a new chance to shine.

If the student is an English learner (EL), can he or she access the information in his or her native language? If the goal of the assignment is to improve English skills, then reading in his or her own language would defeat the purpose. But, if the goal is to understand ideas and use information in a specific way, this alternative route would allow EL students to participate more fully.

This line of learning-objective-focused questioning works for any subject. If students are supposed to be studying history, can they choose to study a person of interest to them within the specific time period? If they are doing a science project, can they choose their own experiment that fits with the overall topic? Could they demonstrate their learning through alternative creative options such as making a video, designing a poster, or writing a story?

Such flexibility takes more organizational skill than traditional, teacher-controlled learning. While students all have to meet the same checkpoints in order to complete the assignment, those different experiments and topics might reach those checkpoints with some variation. The key is to let the project develop while keeping your eye on that underlying learning goal.

Such flexibility requires a strong foundation in content knowledge as well. If groups of students are doing different experiments along the same topic, they will arrive at different questions, each at their own pace. Chances are these questions won't align with the sequence outlined in the textbook. Rather, students will be turning to you for information in the order they need to know it. If you are solid in the content area, students will trust that you will continue to be their safety net as they take new learning risks.

Increased trust is one of the huge positives that arises out of a well-structured, flexible classroom. The more diverse the paths students take to reach your learning objectives, the more opportunities they have to learn from each other. As you work to create a team atmosphere, students help each other on their various projects in appropriate ways: through knowledge, skills, and social support.

If the project is a group project, they have to learn to deal with conflict in positive ways. They learn to trust each other for support, and they learn to trust the instructor to create a clearly defined setting in which their learning style is valued and encouraged.

When the assignment is finally completed, sharing those final projects becomes a powerful opportunity to emphasize the learning journey. Because different students reached the goal differently, sharing these experiences enhances everyone's learning. Often we as teachers are able to learn something new, too.

TAKING THE LONG-TERM VIEW

Teacher flexibility requires clear structure, creative thinking, and a willingness to be surprised. The results, according to those graduate students' pearls of wisdom, are worth it every time.

One of the challenges of flexibility is that it requires us as teachers to take a long-term view of the situation. It's a challenge because so much of teaching happens in the moment and involves our full range of skills and emotions. But there are tremendous benefits: stepping back from the situation where Ray won't talk or Sarah doesn't like to read, we can take a deep breath and ask, "What's the final learning goal here?"

The expectations for student performance are high, but students are allowed many different ways of meeting those expectations.

Over time, increasing flexibility in the classroom can bring about several pleasant changes, both in teaching mentality and in the classroom atmosphere. Teacher flexibility requires you to tap into your creative side. Creative work keeps those staple lessons feeling new and interesting, and the interdependent focus helps you keep thinking outside your own box.

There is a confidence that comes from knowing that the way things were done in the past is okay, but new solutions might be even better. Each time a student finds an alternative way of excelling at a learning task, the more likely it seems that there are still more new solutions to every problem. The more solutions you find for reaching out to students, the easier it becomes to keep finding them.

That kind of creative thinking is empowering for teachers and for students alike. Information is powerful, and you can get it from many different sources beyond the one required textbook. And, when those creative attempts at encouraging student learning fail, there is the opportunity to begin again, knowing more than you did at the start.

The result of this flexible teaching is to flatten the power structure in the classroom. No longer is the teacher the grand purveyor of all knowledge, including the one right way to present the answer. Everyone has the opportunity to lead at some point on some topic or skill. Rather than approaching class from a consumer point of view, everyone can now be a contributor to the learning community. The stakes become higher and the results more relevant.

Allowing students to pursue alternative approaches puts them in control while holding them accountable. If it was their idea to make a model instead of writing a paper, to choose a specific experiment, or to present a biography in rap form, they are the ones who have to live up to the expectations they set. They tend to put more time and energy into the project, working to produce something they can be proud of. The result—the constant, long-term goal—is deeper learning.

Over time, our jobs are made easier by developing an "enough" perspective. Learning is not a competition. There is enough love, hope, success, faith, and joy for everyone. As long as the level of risk stays fun and manageable, there is joy in learning.

Good teachers are lifelong learners, and we want our students to be, as well. The more creative ways we can allow students to meet our expectations, the more fun learning is for all of us.

Chapter Fifteen

Dimensions of Understanding

Imagine going to see the doctor. He asks a series of questions about your symptoms, and in the end he prescribes a new medication. He explains the purpose and the dosage, then asks if you have any questions. So far, all is clear. You pick up the prescription at the pharmacy, where the pharmacist asks you through the window if you have any questions—again, no questions.

The next morning, you wake up thinking, "Wait a minute, was I supposed to take that with food? When should I start decreasing the dosage again?"

You thought you understood the directions. You gave both the doctor and the pharmacist every indication that you understood what they were trying to tell you. But when it came time to apply the directions, you ended up back on the phone with the doctor, just to clarify.

It's tough to know exactly what it means when someone says they understand. Does that mean they get the general concept? That they are able to apply the information? That they are totally lost and are simply nodding and smiling with the hopes that they'll figure it out later?

If you ask a classroom full of students whether they have any questions, their responses likely won't indicate their understanding. It's not cool to say, "No, teacher, I don't get it," in front of everyone. You might get a few socially acceptable questions about what will be on the test and how an assignment should be formatted, but probably nothing more heartfelt than that.

After all, everyone knows that if no one has any questions, you get to move on. You might even get out early. Do the students understand the material in this case? Maybe.

To assess student understanding, the questions you ask need to change. "Do you understand?"—a question with an implied affirmative answer— becomes "*What*" or even "*How* do you understand?" And how they understand has everything to do with the intent of the instructional sequence and learning activities.

Understanding, like learning, comes at multiple levels. Systems theorist Peter Senge put forth a description of these levels in his book, *The Fifth Discipline,* and they are a useful entry point for understanding understanding.

1. Surface-level understanding (an event explanation)

   At this level of understanding, each incident is viewed as an isolated event. The learner's responses are reactionary: something happens, and you do something about it. The context (who, what, when, where, or why) does not come into play in formulating a response. Rather, you "fix" one situation at a time and move on. I had a surface-level understanding of my doctor's orders.

2. Intellectual-level understanding (a pattern of behavior explanation)

   At this level, each incident is viewed as part of a larger pattern. The learner's response is still reactionary, but he or she understands that there is a pattern at play. He or she might understand that "when this happens, then this will most likely follow; these events are either correlated or cause-and-effect, but I know they are somehow related."

3. Dynamical-level understanding (a generative explanation)

   At this level, the learner understands *why* the pattern is occurring in the first place. He or she grasps the context of the incident and knows how he or she fits within that context. The learner's experiences, needs, development, and any pressures he or she might be feeling are all viewed within the overall pattern. Freed to step back and see the big picture, the learner can formulate the best (generative) response for the situation.

Generally speaking, then, all behaviors exist within a pattern of behaviors— and those patterns meet learners' needs. Applying Senge's levels, you can understand classroom behaviors 1) one event at a time, 2) as part of a pattern, or 3) as part of the overall big picture. No matter the level of understanding, behaviors meet the needs of the individual, so telling someone, "Stop doing that!" is not helpful. Rather, as Chapter 2 discusses, that person needs help replacing that behavior with a more effective behavior or pattern of behaviors.

These three levels of understanding can also be applied to *how* we understand things. Ultimately, the understanding questions are these: "What does that understanding allow you to do?" and "How might you demonstrate your depth of understanding?"

Let's turn to the various common types of learning to see what their levels of understanding look like. We'll look at seven different kinds of learning that teachers might aim for in a classroom: concept understanding, context, analysis, critical thinking, application, creativity, and self-knowledge. The more we know about *how* we want students to understand the learning, the more easily we can assess where our students are.

CONCEPT UNDERSTANDING

Do you understand in such a way as to follow a concept?

In order to understand a concept or make a generalization, learners need to have enough experiences with an idea to see the commonalities. As a result, they can place the event along a bell-shaped curve of experiences, judging what is normal or likely.

- Surface level: the experience is the concept. E.g., *When I think of pets, I think of my dog. Pets are dogs.*
- Intellectual level: the student is able to say, "Generally speaking, this concept has these things in common." E.g., *I've noticed that other people have other kinds of pets. Cats, hamsters, fish, and even tarantulas can be pets, too.*
- Dynamical level: the student can speak to general characteristics while incorporating individual exceptions and anomalies. E.g., *I get that animals fulfill a human need for companionship, and I can explain how even uncommon pets fit within the definition.*

CONTEXT

Do you understand in such a way as to place the concept within its context?

Context refers to the who, what, when, where, and why of the idea being studied. Fully understanding context requires interpretation, empathy, and perspective.

- Surface level: the event, person, or concept is described from a current point of view. This is an outside-looking-in perspective. E.g., *The American Revolutionary War began in 1776 and involved the following events . . .*
- Intellectual level: the learner is still an outsider looking in but is able to place the situation accurately within the time period. E.g., *The following events and beliefs, seen throughout the colonies and around the world, contributed to the start of the American Revolution . . .*

- Dynamical level: nuances are clear and explicit. The student is able to describe the event, person, or idea from an "at that time, at that place, in that situation . . ." perspective. He or she sees the concept from an insider's point of view. E.g., *I can imagine what was at stake for the signers of the Declaration of Independence. I can explain why they made the decisions they made.*

ANALYSIS

Do you understand in such a way as to conduct an analysis?
    Analysis refers to the ability to break the whole into its parts and to identify the relationship(s) between the pieces.

- Surface level: the pieces are correctly identified and named. E.g., *These are the parts of a bicycle.*
- Intellectual level: the pieces are correctly identified and named. Each piece is described with appropriate detail in terms of its structure and/or function. E.g., *Here is how this part of the bicycle works. Here is how that part works.*
- Dynamical level: the pieces are correctly identified and named, and each piece is described with appropriate detail in terms of its structure and/or function. Furthermore, the pieces are described in relationship to each other. There is an emphasis upon the interactions or interconnections between the pieces in order to make up the whole. E.g., *This is how each of the pieces works together to create an efficient system of motion.*

CRITICAL THINKING

Do you understand in such a way as to think critically about the concept?
    Critical thinking refers to the ability to rank or order the pieces in terms of importance or other specified criteria. To make decisions based upon field specifics, the learner must be able to identify and use criteria defined by field experts.

- Surface level: rankings/decisions are made based upon prior individual-based experiences. While this may move beyond the level of like or dislike, choices are still mainly based on opinion. E.g., *Pizza is yummy. The school cafeteria should serve pizza for lunch.*
- Intellectual level: rankings/decisions are made with references to past experiences of self as well as others. E.g., *The school cafeteria should serve pizza for lunch because many students like it. More students buy hot lunch on pizza days.*

- Dynamical level: rankings/decisions are made using field-specific, expert criteria. E.g., *If the school cafeteria serves pizza, the meal will have the following nutritional content. Let's consider whether that meets the dietary needs of the student body.*

APPLICATION

Do you understand in such a way as to apply the concept to other situations?

Application refers to the ability to use knowledge and skills in appropriate, novel, and difficult situations.

- Surface level: the learner is able to follow a prescribed set of procedures in order to complete a task. E.g., *I can follow this list of instructions to build a rocket.*
- Intellectual level: the learner is able to follow a prescribed set of procedures. He or she identifies the need to learn or modify new skills or knowledge in order to complete the task. E.g., *I can follow this list of instructions to build a rocket. Step three is unfamiliar to me, so I will look it up and learn how to complete that task.*
- Dynamical level: the learner is able to create his or her own set of procedures, refine the necessary skills, and learn new information in order to complete the task. E.g., *I understand that rockets work this way. If I can get these pieces to work together in this specific way, I should have a darn cool rocket.*

CREATIVITY

Do you understand in such a way as to treat the concept creatively?

Creativity allows a person to combine pieces that have not been combined before or to see things from new and different perspectives. Creativity requires fluency (a measure of the number of ideas generated), flexibility (the number of categories of ideas generated), originality (unique ideas), and elaboration (the ability to modify ideas in order to meet the needs of the task at hand).

- Surface level: one or more of the following creative aspects are evident (fluency, flexibility, originality, elaboration), but they do not lead to new solutions or perspectives. E.g., *After considering my technological needs and the various ways I might address them, I wrote this computer program. I did not invent anything new, but it works!*

- Intellectual level: the learner is able to create a complete and robust modification of an existing concept to solve the problem at hand. E.g., *I've analyzed how this computer program works, considered all the ways it might run, and redesigned it to make it better.*
- Dynamical level: the learner demonstrates the highest level of fluency, flexibility, originality, and elaboration. Pieces are combined that have not been combined before or a new perspective has been utilized to solve the problem at hand. E.g., *Because I approached the issue in an entirely new way, I was able to invent a program that has changed the way we use computers.*

SELF-KNOWLEDGE

Do you understand in such a way as to incorporate it into your worldview?

Self-knowledge refers to the point when students take responsibility for their learning and make it their own. At this level, learners recognize that they own their own thoughts, actions, and belief systems.

- Surface level: the learner is beginning to be aware of how his or her thoughts, actions, and belief systems impact his or her learning or view of reality. E.g., *I live in Small Town, Wisconsin. My experiences may be different from someone who lives in a big city.*
- Intellectual level: the learner is beginning to choose what he or she will learn from each learning episode. E.g., *Living in Small Town, Wisconsin, I see a lot of hunting, ice fishing, and cheese curds. I'm going to embrace these things (or not) as part of where I'm growing up.*
- Dynamical level: the learner owns the interactions between his or her personal thoughts, actions, and belief systems. E.g., *My thoughts and expectations about the world have been formed by my upbringing in Small Town, Wisconsin. I can celebrate how my upbringing has made me who I am today, and I can recognize where there are gaps in my experience.*

UNDERSTANDING IN THE CLASSROOM

Stephen Covey, in his book, *The 7 Habits of Highly Effective People*, states that you can have *anything* you want, just not *everything* you want. Certainly this is true for the classroom. Students are not going to achieve dynamical levels of understanding on all of the above dimensions of understanding, but they can get there on some of them.

The type of understanding you want your students to achieve determines the learning activities, sequence, questions, and answers you choose to use. As always, the more explicit you can be about the learning you want to see, the better.

At the dynamical level, learning is always seen from a systems point of view. In other words, everything is connected. Nothing exists in isolation. As we'll talk about in Chapter 19, changing one thing in a system ultimately impacts everything else. The learner who understands these connections becomes incredibly empowered and powerful in decision-making.

The wonderful news is that we as teachers are free to start small. Pick one type of understanding to focus on at a time. Model it for the class; value it with the necessary time, effort, and resources; and assess it explicitly. Remember that only the learner can choose when and how to own that new learning.

Then, step back and let the students share what they know.

Chapter Sixteen

Student Learning Data

It's Always Perfect!

We collect student learning data all the time. From state testing to Positive Behavioral Interventions and Supports (PBIS) to Response to Intervention (RtI) models, teachers are constantly amassing data on student learning. We grade homework, quizzes, and tests. We utilize checkpoints to monitor how students are doing in our class. State and national exams gather their own data.

And, even when we don't have the grade book out, we are constantly assessing student learning through both verbal and nonverbal means. Are they answering questions correctly? Signaling with their body language and tone that they are ready to move on?

There is no shortage of data. The question is, how do we use the data we already have to inform our practice and increase student learning?

Often we don't make full use out of the data we collect. There are all sorts of good excuses: collecting and analyzing data can be difficult and time consuming, on top of schedules that are already filled to the brim. Our own college and ongoing educations don't always provide the training we need to handle the analysis.

Or, given today's high-stakes emphasis on test scores, we use data selectively, focusing on the results that make us look or feel good, such as how many students earned As.

We can all point to the tests that don't measure the full extent of student learning: why judge ourselves based on those scores? And really, how much more does a busy teacher have to do?

This chapter is not about doing more. It's about refocusing on what we already have—starting with tests, and what they really show us.

The words "test" and "assessment" are practically synonymous, but in reality tests are used more for sorting than learning. They categorize students as high, average, and low performers, ideally arranged in a bell curve.

In fact, it's hard to trust a test that doesn't give us bell curve results. What would you make of a test that produced nearly all As? Would it demonstrate that all the students learned the material really well, or was it simply too easy of a test? It's hard to tell.

In memorization-focused tests, the results matter little for learning, anyway. By the time the tests are graded, you've moved on to the next unit. And, since the facts learned in the last unit are not connected to future learning, they don't affect the current classroom environment. If students didn't learn the information, then that will be the problem of the next teacher the next time the subject comes up.

The result has a rather win-lose feel to it; students either won and did well on the test, or they didn't (and lost). Either way, the course moves on.

High-stakes testing, such as standardized testing, is problematic in its own right when it comes to assessment. Here the emphasis on sorting over learning is even clearer. Normed to fit a bell curve, these tests rank our schools against the national average but tell us little about what our students actually know.

Teachers don't even see the specific questions to which the final results correspond. It wouldn't matter if we did: by the time we get back the tests results from our class, we are already working with another group.

When it comes to what we do with the results, these tests are of limited use for improving learning because they are viewed as the ceiling for learning, rather than the threshold. The results tell us how close to the top students are, not what they might be on the brink of achieving.

Let's go back to classroom assessment, then, and to the tests and quizzes teachers control from creation to final grade.

What is assessment, beyond norms and bell curves? Assessment is always a comparison between the results you expect and the student work (learning data) you receive. The point of assessment is to improve student learning and to improve teaching choices. That happens when we connect the results of our assessments to our curriculum learning goals and our lesson plans. It's a cycle of learning.

When we assess students, we are saying, "Here's what I think they should understand, and here's what they really got." Regardless of the results, we learn something that is helpful in teaching. The results show us whether we taught a unit effectively, and what specific areas we might want to focus on next time.

Data, then, is a communication tool. It says, "I said this, and they interpreted it this way. I did x, and from that they learned y." Because the learning is set up as a spiral, we are released from the pressure of having students "get it" all at once. We'll keep coming back to the same key ideas over and over again, each time in developmentally appropriate ways, with more depth and complexity. Each time, students make more connections, and our expectations rise to keep the work appropriately challenging.

The goal is to have more students learning more content, with more depth and more connections—for us teachers to become more effective with more students.

PERFECT DATA

Student learning data is always perfect, because it always communicates something to you about the effectiveness of your teaching. It either tells you

- that things went exactly as you expected, with your lesson being right on the mark, or
- what you might need to change or modify. These changes might take place in your lesson plans, teaching strategies, expectations, or time frames. Unclear data might communicate that your assessment techniques need to change. Regardless, you now know what you have to work on next.

Keep it simple. Too much data gets overwhelming, and too many changes to teaching at once can leave you feeling as though you are constantly reinventing the wheel, with little chance to test which change(s) made the difference. Put student learning data together in simple ways that you can connect to your teaching and learning choices.

For a sense of the ways that data can be analyzed, we turn to charts.

Table 16.1 Test Data

Grades	A	B	C	D	F
Number of Students	3	8	12	4	3

There are multiple ways of interpreting this data:

1. This test did a good job of sorting students. It is clear that some students "get it" and some do not. There is a clear bell curve here, with more than two-thirds of the class understanding 75 percent of the material.
2. There are seven students who are clearly struggling with this material. Hopefully they will do better on the next test or chapter.

3. This is unacceptable. This lesson will have to be retaught because seven students out of thirty clearly did not "get it."

There are, of course, many other interpretations. You might be naturally drawn to see the good news in this data or the bad. How well you know your students and the content you were asking them to learn are also important factors that will influence your response and determine what you do with the information.

The following chart gets more specific, tallying incorrect answers on individual test questions.

Table 16.2 Item Analysis for Test Data

Item Number	Number of Students Answering Incorrectly	Item Number	Number of Students Answering Incorrectly
1	3	13	22
2	8	14	16
3	4	15	7
4	0	16	3
5	20	17	4
6	7	18	2
7	3	19	13
8	6	20	15
9	1	21	4
10	5	22	6
11	2	23	2
12	3	24	8

There are multiple ways of interpreting this data:

1. On items 4, 9, 11, 12, 16, 18, and 23, students did very well. Maybe those items were too easy.
2. Items 5, 13, 14, 19, and 20 were problematic—too many students did not "get" what the question was asking. This might be a case of unclear wording, or it might signal that they did not learn that material.
3. It's necessary to look more closely at the items students did very well on (4, 9, 11, 12, 16, 18, and 23) and very poorly on (5, 13, 14, 19, and 20) and connect those to lesson plans when teaching those concepts. What worked well? What needs more work?

This kind of reflection, while it might take some time, is helpful in multiple ways. Connecting test answers back to lesson plans not only helps you teach that unit more effectively next time but also helps you teach this particular student group more effectively now. As the term continues and patterns emerge, this kind of data analysis will get quicker and easier.

There are many other interpretations, depending on how well you know your students and the content you were asking them to learn.

This third chart evaluates student projects using a rubric. Rubrics were distributed at the beginning of the task. Four is the highest mark, while 0 is the lowest.

Table 16.3 Student Learning Data from a Classroom Task Evaluated with Criteria and Rubrics

Number of Students Achieving Each Score

Rubric Scores	4	3	2	1	0
Criteria #1	14	12	3	0	1
Criteria #2	12	10	7	0	1
Criteria #3	4	14	10	0	2
Criteria #4	1	2	16	10	1

There are multiple ways of interpreting this data:

1. Students clearly understood criteria 1 and 2. After evaluating their learning task, it's clear that modeling and practicing allowed students to grasp those two concepts.
2. Criteria 3 was more problematic—although many students achieved "basic understanding" (2s) there were very few 4s. Students need to show more than basic understanding on this important subject. It's worth looking again at how that criterion was taught.
3. Even though criteria 4 may be problematic, because students are allowed the chance to redo this task, this result is not troubling. Criteria 4 is very complex, and students need more time and experiences developing this idea. The majority have the basic concept. We will continue to revisit this idea and have more practice opportunities as the semester progresses.

There are, of course, many other interpretations, depending on how well you know your students and the content you were asking them to learn.

As you get more refined and sophisticated in your analysis, you can use student learning data for smaller and smaller groups. You might break down assessment results by gender, learning preference, developmental ability, special education needs, English language proficiency, socioeconomic status, and so on, depending on what you want to focus on. Below is the same learning data as in Figure 3, broken into smaller categories to allow for analysis of student response by gender.

Table 16.4 Student Learning Data from a Classroom Task Evaluated with Criteria and Rubrics, with Males (M) and Females (F) Separated

Number of Students Achieving Each Score

Rubric Scores	4	3	2	1	0
Criteria #1	8 M / 6 F	6 M / 6 F	1 M / 2 F	—	1 M / —
Criteria #2	4 M / 8 F	4 M / 6 F	7 M / —	—	1 M / —
Criteria #3	— / 4 F	8 M / 6 F	6 M / 4 F	—	2 M / —
Criteria #4	1 M / —	1 M / 1 F	13 M / 3F	— / 10 F	1 M / —

There are multiple ways of interpreting this data:

1. The females in the class understood criteria 2 better than the males.
2. Males understood criteria 4 better than the females.
3. Criteria 1 seems to be gender-neutral, and criteria 3 seems to be OK.

There are, of course, many other interpretations, depending on how well you know your students and the content you were asking them to learn. In column zero, for example, it makes a difference whether there was one male who failed all the categories—indicating a problem with a particular student—or whether different males are represented here.

These charts are a clear, visual way to break down student learning data so that you can connect it back to your lesson plans. It took less than five minutes to make each one. Seeing numbers instead of a list of names in a grade book helps a teacher step back from the personalities of the classroom and consider trends.

Now that you have that information, you can decide how it aligns with your expectations and what you will do next—whether you will move on, reteach a concept, or modify future lessons.

EMBRACING THE LEARNING CYCLE

Thinking of student learning data as a vital part of a learning cycle alleviates the blame that sometimes comes from assessments that did not meet expectations. Test results are no longer the end of the road, marked with signs that say, "They didn't get it," or "I messed up this lesson."

Student learning data communicates to you and to your students, and your analysis of that data equips you as you write further curricula. The cycle looks like this:

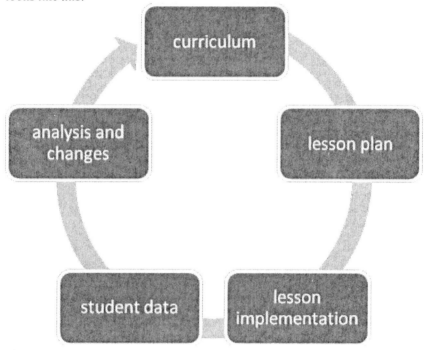

Figure 16.1

The key is to use student learning data in such a way as to help you see what you need to learn next. You might want to chart your data to examine specific strategies for underperforming groups or individuals. You might want the data to show you how much students understand or how relevant they are finding the material. The data could demonstrate whether checkpoints are working or could respond to other specific choices you made.

Whatever you want to learn, keep it simple. Let this tool support you in what you want to learn as you move on through the year.

Teachers do not automatically get better with time. A thirteen-year study done among university professors found that student evaluations stayed pretty much the same year after year. (Practice makes permanent!) What did improve student evaluations was focused, data-driven guidance from a mentor teacher or group.[1]

If you are able to be part of a professional learning community where teachers share ideas and work together to improve student learning, the kinds of charts shown in this chapter are perfect discussion material. With this data, the conversation no longer begins and ends with, "I feel like this could have gone better." Instead, the results of your assessments allow you to make data-driven decisions. Sometimes the numbers show that the lesson went better than you thought!

Student learning data need not be for professional eyes only. Sharing these charts with students, if done in such a way as to avoid finger-pointing, provides an opportunity to debrief learning with students. Discussing data is a perfect platform for clarifying expectations and modeling what learning looks like. The result of such conversations is a sharing of power, with the students adding their own expectations for future learning.

Such an activity represents an enormous shift from a teacher vs. student, authoritative handing down of grades. (Note: grades don't change as a result of this discussion, but students better understand what grades mean.) Working as a team, you can set a common vision or purpose for the next learning unit.

Rather than having students feel like the best they can do is meet expectations on that next big evaluation, they may come to see those expectations as the minimum bar for work: the threshold for excellent performance, rather than the ceiling they are trying to reach.

As the learning cycle image above demonstrates, assessment is not a tool you can use once and then discard. The challenge that keeps us on our toes while teaching is that the audience is always changing. Class makeup shifts from year to year, meaning that what worked perfectly for the last group may not strike a balance for the next. Throughout the year, too, students grow developmentally.

They will change as they learn, and the resulting student learning data will keep you abreast of those changes.

NOTE

1. Marsh, Herbert W. "Do University Teachers Become More Effective with Experience? A Multilevel Growth Model of Students' Evaluations of Teaching over 13 Years." *Journal of Educational Psychology* 99, no.4 (2007): 775–790.

Chapter Seventeen

Including Parents/Guardians

Teaching wouldn't be such a big deal if we only had to deal with students. We also have to work with other teachers, school administrators, board members, and the toughest group of all: parents. Generally speaking, teachers just don't know what to do with them.

For the most part our interactions with parents are stilted. We meet them on our turf, in our timeframes, and we have power over their children—real power. Power to give poor grades, power to give time after school, and power to make or break their children's day—even their future. This power can make some parents/guardians feel uncomfortable. Sometimes parents/guardians approach teacher meetings feeling like they have to assert themselves in order to ensure their child's needs are met.

What's more, all parents/guardians have been in schools. They are products of the very system that is educating their children. That means they will tend to approach the school from their perspective. If they loved music, then why doesn't their child? If they hated math, shouldn't their kids hate it, too? If they were a bullying victim, isn't everyone out to get their child?

And if they had the worst social studies teacher ever when they were in school, and you happen to teach social studies, it's entirely possible that their experience will flavor your conversations. In short, parents/guardians have beliefs about the schooling experience that are both real and true—to them.

As the child progresses from grade to grade, schooling gets scarier and scarier to parents/guardians. In elementary schools they are frequently invited into the classroom and can help with school assignments at home. They can read to their children or do flashcards to help with math and memorization. Chances are, they will know a little about the content that their children are supposed to be learning.

It is also clear that in most elementary classrooms the teachers know a lot about their children. Teachers spend nearly the entire school day with the same children, and their knowledge is evidenced in report cards. Four times a year, those documents provide parents/guardians with lots of information about how their child is developing, what their child needs to work on next, and in what areas their child seems to exhibit excellence. Report cards in lower grades are about growth and development rather than sorting and judging.

Starting around fourth grade, the report card changes—and so do parent/guardian-teacher interactions. Students now get grades that represent their performance within the class; it becomes the parents'/guardians' responsibility to check homework, provide resources, and make sure that their child successfully completes what the teacher has assigned. Student failure begins to look like parent failure.

The higher the grade, the less securely firm-footed parents/guardians may start to feel in approaching teachers. The teachers are less familiar: parents/guardians may only meet them once in a year, and they are probably hearing less about them from their teens at home. Teachers in higher grades spend only one class period around their students, meaning those teachers may no longer be an expert on each child.

If a content area is outside of a parent's field of work, he or she may not have seen the material since he or she was in high school. The parent/guardian may not remember it well enough to help with homework.

If their children are having trouble at a higher grade, you can imagine that some parents/guardians might approach teachers with an "us vs. them" mentality. Teachers might feel the same way.

Here is one of the key ideas when working with concerned parents/guardians: they tend to view their child's successes and failures as their own. *When my child fails—I fail. When my child succeeds, it means I must have done something right.* That is the parent way. The stakes are high. And the more the parents/guardians are involved in their child's life, the more deeply those feelings go.

Not all parents/guardians are invested in the success of their children, unfortunately. Some parents/guardians, for a variety of reasons, will always be missing in action. This chapter likely won't apply to them. But, for the parents/guardians who are involved—the ones who are contacting you about their children—seeing the situation from their point of view is a helpful starting point for collaboration. Working with parents/guardians makes your job easier.

GREAT EXPECTATIONS

Setting aside school expectations for a moment, parents/guardians take on a natural progression of roles as their children grow. Parents/guardians begin (ideally) as the child's number one fan and advocate. Their role is to provide for and defend the child. Like a mama bear whose cubs are threatened, parents/guardians flip into defense mode when their child's safety or well-being is at stake. They want the best for their children, and it helps to show that you as a teacher want the same.

As children grow, parents/guardians take on additional roles. They become teachers of rules, morals, and beliefs. They pass on views about life, including opinions on diversity, money, education, opposite gender, work ethic, respect, responsibility, and so on. Some parents/guardians act as though the entire burden for educating their child is in the hands of the teacher; they may not realize the extent to which they are teaching their child every day.

Schools frequently assign parents/guardians additional roles for which they may or may not feel prepared. Starting when their children first begin to have homework, parents/guardians become the teacher's assistant. They help with content (if they can), provide resources, and help their children organize and plan their time. They might take on the role of homework heavy, telling their kids to get it done even if they see no relevance to the homework task.

They are also called upon to be communicators between school and home life, following through on what the school or teacher says they need to do if they want their child to succeed—no matter what they believe or have the capacity to do. In other words, parents/guardians are expected to support the work of the teacher without necessarily knowing anything about how the teacher has structured the classroom or why assignments are given.

The school's expectations are evident in the types of invitations parents/guardians receive from schools. Once a child enters middle school, the types of events parents are expected to attend change. Here is a common list: parent-teacher conferences, meet-the-teacher night, electronic homework sites, band/orchestra/choir concerts, theater productions, and sporting events. What is conspicuously absent from the list are classroom invitations that showcase what the students have actually learned.

> *Story: I used to teach one or two low-ability classes per semester when I was a high school science teacher. During parent-teacher conferences, I almost never had a busy schedule. As I got to thinking about it, I realized why those parents/guardians did not attend. Why give of your time, effort, and resources to hear about the failures of your child? How different will it be from what you heard last year, the year before that, or the year before that?*

You know they are not doing well in school, but how do you change it?
And is there nothing good or worthwhile about their child that you have
noticed? No redeeming value? No joy in who they are?
They chose not to attend because success was rarely an option.

What is clearly lacking in most parent-teacher relationships is any type of partnership perspective. Just as with the students, power impacts relationships, and the most powerful place to build relationships begins with building interpersonal understanding.

WHAT PARENTS/GUARDIANS WANT

As with any collaborative relationship, working with parents/guardians requires consideration of their point of view. The following is a list of what many parents/guardians want from their schools and their children's teachers:

1. *Parents/guardians want communication—the two-way kind.* They want you to ask about their children: how they learn, what they are good at, what they might need to focus on to be successful, other activities they participate in, siblings, responsibilities, sense of humor, and other topics. Many parents/guardians are dying to tell you something special about their children. Unfortunately, most teachers do not ask.

They also want to hear you talk about how their children are special in your classroom: what they do well, how they interact socially, any talents that might not have surfaced at home, and so on. Parents/guardians want to hear way more positives than negatives, if possible. They want to know (deep in their hearts) that the child they have entrusted to your care is known and cared for as an individual.

Believe it or not, most parents/guardians also are aware of the weaknesses of their child, and most frequently do not know what to do about it. They are not trained teachers, or counselors, or school psychologists. What they know about teaching and learning is most frequently a result of their own schooling experiences (think about that for just one minute) or how they were raised.

What parents/guardians want is to be viewed as a partner in their child's learning.

2. *Parents/guardians want to have their beliefs accepted.* You cannot change anyone else's belief systems, certainly not those of parents/guardians who you see rather infrequently. You need to understand that those beliefs are also very visible in their children. When you criticize a child's beliefs, more frequently than not, those are the parents'/guardians' beliefs, as well.

What parents/guardians want is to let their children share their beliefs in a safe environment. A powerful strategy in your classroom is to teach creativity and acknowledge the power of seeing the same thing from multiple perspectives.

3. *Parents/guardians want support for their child.* Most parents/guardians do not have training in teaching or child development, but you do. Your ideas and strategies can help parents/guardians to be supportive as their child grows.

As fitting with the situation, some parents/guardians will truly appreciate hearing what is "normal" for any particular age group. They might want to hear ideas about physical changes and how they might choose to respond, as well as ideas about reading, homework, emotional support, encouragement, perseverance, and excellence. Help them be the most effective advocate for their child that they can be.

Parents/guardians need help in doing the right thing for their children. Not all parents/guardians do, but some. Being an educator means partnering with parents/guardians to do the best they can do—which may, in fact, make your job easier in the long run. Providing references, resources, lists, ideas, checklists, or names of others can build the relationship with struggling parents/ guardians.

Anyone who has children knows that they don't come with guidebooks— as much as we might want one. For parents/guardians trying to do their best at this challenging role, what they ultimately want is to understand their children as they grow and to provide appropriate help.

4. *Parents/guardians want their children to be successful.* Structure your classroom so that student success is the norm. While many view the teacher's role as one of sorting out the top students from the bottom, the majority of teachers view teaching as their top goal. Students achieve success when they learn.

Believing you can be successful allows you to give of your time, effort, and resources so that success is more likely in the future (a positive spiral). Success is the number one motivator. Conversely, if you do not believe you can be successful—they why bother trying at all?

As we talked about in Chapter 8 ("Setting Appropriate Expectations"), seeking student success does not mean making the class easier. High, developmentally appropriate expectations are important; success means more when the task is challenging. As you get to know your students, you can encourage them to play to their strengths, helping them successfully meet your learning goals.

5. *Parents/guardians want to see their children shine*. The emphasis here is on the verb; more than knowing intellectually how their children are doing in school, parents/guardians want to *see* it. Consider inviting parents/guardians to attend content-specific showcase events. Using an open house format, invite parents/guardians once a quarter to witness what their students have learned. This is not a teacher-directed evening that lasts forever; it is a one-hour open house led by the students themselves.

They can showcase something they have created, built, written, discovered, composed, or invented. What is important to remember is to have every child out front and center at some point during the event.

The classic musical, *The Music Man* , gives a great example of this desire. The story follows a charming con artist who sells instruments for young boys to start bands, then leaves town with the money before anyone realizes that he knows nothing about music. At the end he gets caught, and the parents// guardians threaten to tar and feather him if the kids don't show what they learned.

So they begin to play, and it is terrible. The noise gets worse and worse, and the Music Man thinks he is doomed for sure—until one mother stands up and yells, "Play it for me, Johnny!"

Inviting students to show what they have learned can be a scary occurrence. Teachers worry about the quality of the performance, but for many parents/guardians, seeing their child out front and center is more important than the quality you might wish for.

What parents/guardians want is evidence that their children are special!

Parents/guardians give their children to schools every day, hoping that someone will love and care for them as individuals in their stead. They know their children are not perfect. By demonstrating that you know their children well, you establish common ground.

Traditional parent/guardian-teacher relationships have a power differential that most frequently stifles open communication. The result is adults talking at each other, neither listening nor acknowledging what the other really cares about. And while there is no guarantee that you will see eye to eye about methods, when you focus on what parents/guardians want, it becomes easier to work *with* them in order to reach your common goal: the best possible education for their children.

Chapter Eighteen

From Classroom to Community

Picture this: you are a student on the night before school starts. You will have a brand-new teacher (or several) and new classmates. Perhaps you will have to learn a new locker combination and navigate your way to all your classrooms. You might be worried, excited, mourning the loss of summer, or all of the above. To make matters worse, you've learned that your closest friends will not be in your class(es).

One question strikes you with a sudden note of worry: "Who will I sit with at lunch?"

In class, your teacher will determine where you sit and probably whom you work with, but lunch—that's another story. You picture yourself standing in the middle of the room holding your tray, everyone's eyes on you (or their backs turned, whichever scares you more), all making it clear that you are not part of the group. What if you end up eating all alone?

Picture the same cafeteria now, from a teacher's point of view. All the students have eventually managed to sit somewhere and are talking and eating with their usual deafening roar. No one is getting food thrown at them at the moment. Everything seems okay.

Is that a community? Whether a student would say yes or no would depend in large part on whether he or she was able to sit with a friend group. From the teacher's point of view, well, that depends on how well you know those students. Look closer. Who's talking? Who's *not* talking? Who would *never* talk to whom unless you made them?

Communities do not happen automatically.

In the classroom, where there are fewer students and ostensibly a common goal—to learn—communities are not a given. After all, in a traditional classroom, learning is presented as an individual or a competitive effort, not a communal one. For older students in traditional, teacher-led classrooms, it's entirely possible to go the whole school year without speaking to some people in the room.

Research shows that having students work in small groups helps create community. Students who dislike speaking in large groups are more comfortable among a few of their peers, and they have greater opportunity to voice their opinions.

All that is true, if you set up small groups carefully, with clear guidelines to encourage discussion. If you let students choose their own groups, students will work with their friends and/or the people sitting next to them, every single time. We are creatures of habit, all of us.

Communities do not form unless you take the time and effort to form them.

A community says, "We're in this together." The people involved have a sense of belonging and buy-in. When one person fails in a well-functioning community, others step in to provide support. The community works well together to meet its common goals, and in doing so it meets the needs of its individuals. That is what keeps an individual returning: a belief that you are known and accepted for who you are.

Communities are very functional groups, and they can form around any common bond. Sports teams, music ensembles, theater troupes, housemates, and workplaces can all be communities—or not, depending on how effectively they work together.

Think of the *Ocean's Eleven* or *Mission Impossible* films: faced with a seemingly impossible task, the groups work well together in both cases because each individual has unique skills that he or she contributes in order to reach a common goal. Every person is important, no matter how large or small the role. If the computer guy working behind the scenes can't hack into the mainframe, if the lookout falls asleep or the leader's planning is faulty, everybody fails. If they all work together, everyone shares the credit.

Highly functional groups demonstrate the following characteristics:

- There is a clear purpose that is shared and explicitly stated.
- People choose to participate (some even have to compete for the opportunity).
- Multiple roles exist within the overall task, allowing everyone to contribute.
- The end product is public.
- Everyone is known as an individual.
- There is a positive group association.
- All succeed or all fail together.

Individuals choose to participate in these groups out of their own interest, and what keeps them involved is the fact that the group values their contribution toward a clearly defined end goal. This usually means people are more committed to give their time, effort, and resources to ensure group success.

In an effective small group, the implication is that everyone needs to learn for the group to be successful. Individual learning is appreciated by the group because one person's work makes everyone's jobs easier. The result is both individual and group accountability.

Imagine how different a traditional classroom is from those characteristics:

- The purpose is unknown by most participants.
- Students have little to no choice(s).
- Everyone competes for the same role of top student.
- Any end product is for classroom eyes only.
- It is possible and probable that many in the class are invisible.
- There is little-to-no group association as a class.
- It matters little if someone fails; rather, it is the norm.

In a traditional classroom, learning is seen as an individual task. If the person next to you in class doesn't get it, who cares (as long as he doesn't slow everybody else down by asking too many questions)? In fact, because most teachers limit the number of As given, one student's success may be viewed as less success for the others in the class.

Why does it matter if classrooms are communities? How can they look more like the first list? After all, students are legally required to be there, and there are only so many choices a teacher can allow them—right? Students may have to be physically present, but being part of a community helps them to be mentally and emotionally invested. And that can lead to deeper learning.

The characteristics of highly functional groups meet people's needs for power, love, freedom, and fun. Individuals have power because they are able to contribute, and their contributions are necessary. The group needs them to do their task well in order to succeed, and that sense of being good at something motivates further learning.

Positive group association provides for love and belonging, because each person is appreciated and known individually. Freedom comes into play because each individual gets to choose whether or not to participate. (There is always the option to sit out the project and reap the consequences: a failing grade.)

What about fun? Being involved in a group that truly works well together *can be* fun. Succeeding at a task that is appropriately challenging is gratifying. Because individual learning is tied to what the group needs to do to improve, the teacher is happy, too.

GROUP THINK (THE GOOD KIND)

How do you allow students to make choices and feel ownership in a classroom environment? One way to put choice in students' hands is to allow them to create the group rules that everyone will follow. (We talked about choice on a curricular level in Chapter 14.)

Coming up with participation rules is common at the beginning of adult training sessions as well as classes, and participants are usually quick to propose all the rules a teacher could want. They tend to list such excellent requirements as "respect others," "wait your turn to speak," and other variants on the golden rule. The list of rules serves as a contract, and participants then agree to adhere to the rules that they themselves have created.

The only downside to this activity is that any participant, save for very young students, has been in school long enough to list classroom rules without truly thinking about them. We all know that we are supposed to raise our hands before speaking. That, in itself, does not ensure community.

An alternate way to get students thinking about community is to do a Reverse Brainstorming exercise, in which students consider how a given situation could be made worse. The question here would be, "How would we go about designing a classroom that would never exhibit any community characteristics at all?" In debriefing the exercise afterwards, you can turn the negatives ("ignore what others say," "hurt people's feelings," "don't show up") into positive attributes, allowing students to see the usual list of rules in a new way.

In the course of Reverse Brainstorming, words such as "more" and "less" are lethal indicators. If students populate their lists with recommendations like "waste even more time at the start of class" or "given even less positive feedback," that is a sign that these problems exist already. Debriefing allows the group to address these issues that already exist and, hopefully, fix them.

> *Story: In training future teachers, my co-instructors and I stress that everybody needs to contribute in order to create a learning community. We discuss the importance of community at the beginning of the year. This year, we offered suggestions for different ways each student could contribute and encouraged them to come up with their own.*

Our students came up with some surprisingly creative ideas. Two students decided to serve as greeters, and they greeted every person by name at the start of every class meeting. We had a weather person, a homework clarifier, a wellness tip-of-the-day giver, a daily inspirational quote finder.

I could not have predicted how much individual contributions would bene-fit the class as a whole. When a student was not in class, the others noticed. "Where's the weather report?" they would ask. Of all the roles students as-signed themselves, having classroom greeters made the most difference. If students arrived before the classroom greeter got in—no joke—they would walk out of the room and come back later so they could be welcomed by name.

When you know someone is going to greet you by name, you show up. When you know someone is counting on your contribution, you put in the work. A community of supportive individuals allows for a safer environment in which to experiment—even fail dramatically—and learn.

CREATING COMMUNITY, STEP BY STEP

Creating a community is a journey. Getting there happens in stages.

The first stage is what Tuckman[1] calls pseudo-community. It's what often happens with generally nice people who don't know each other well begin working together. Everyone gets along fine, because no one ventures away from the safe, surface-level topics of discussion. There's plenty of smiling and nodding, but very little sense that people know you for who you are.

The next step, chaos, ignites when someone in the group says or does something that challenges the system. Political opinions come out. A person voices her values, and those who disagree must figure out how to respond. The result feels like chaos, and it can leave some members thinking, "What happened? Everyone got along so well before!" That chaotic statement can actually be good for the group, because it can lead others to verbalize the "unsafe" ideas they have, too.

Of course, that chaotic statement is only helpful if the group is able to respond with mature and honest discussion, which is the third stage. Called emptying, it's the stage when people voice what they truly believe. People's deepest thoughts are out on the table, and you get to see more clearly and deeply who the others are around you.

The final stage is true community. As a result of your honest discussions, you have a sense of shared understanding. This is not to say that chaos will never enter the group again; it likely will, but repeated emptying brings the group closer each time.

Put another way, the four stages are forming, storming, norming, and performing.[2] Forming refers to the opening stages. Storming results when someone makes people question or disagree. In norming, the group asks, "How will we agree to get along?" When a group is performing, it is functioning openly and in sync.

These steps are not for the faint of heart. Likely, you've been involved in a group that's been stuck forming or storming, unable to move on to the next step. Underlying the stages are the following five key ideas.[3]

1. Trust. Group members must have emotional bank accounts with each other, which they can draw upon to survive the turmoil that is part of the learning journey. Trust starts to develop during the pseudo-community stage, and it is what encourages people to begin voicing their opinions in the first place. When chaos hits, members are willing to talk it out before walking out on the relationships.

2. Conflict management. Conflict is part of any community. How it is viewed and handled (in the emptying stage) will determine whether the group fragments or grows close relationships. Whether you are maintaining a marriage or controlling a classroom, conflict management skills are a huge determiner of your success.

3. Commitment. The journey toward community is not easy; it is, in fact, far easier not to be involved than to develop true community. Commitment must be an open, discussable fact of group life. That's because commitment is more nuanced than all-or-nothing involvement. Peter Senge outlines the following spectrum from most involved to least: committed, enrolled, compliant, apathetic, and noncompliant.[4] In each of the five levels, the person is still showing up, but only a committed person is actively, continually contributing to the group.

4. Accountability. Because the members of the group trust each other and are committed, they can hold each other to their promises. Accountability allows one member to say to another, "You said you'd do this; where is it?" in a loving way, without anyone feeling attacked or nagged. Rather, each person is held by the group to be his or her best self.

5. Focus on results. The end product, whether it is a sports game, a theater performance, or a class of learners, must trump personal relationships. There must be enough trust and personal responsibility so that members views feedback as a learning opportunity rather than a personal attack.

BACK TO SCHOOL

By now it should be clear that transitioning from a traditional classroom to a learning community represents a tremendous paradigm shift. You won't get there overnight, but a series of small changes can make a big difference. In order to make the transition into a community of learners, there are several things you can do to lay the groundwork.

First and foremost, you can create a safe environment. It must be an atmosphere where students feel they can put their actual thoughts and beliefs out in the open for others to view. With proper safety nets in place, students feel free to make learningful mistakes.

People generally do not choose to fail; this fact must be acknowledged in the class, and the assignment and grading structures must back up your words. If the assignment stresses creativity and experimentation, for example, then creativity and effort should be more heavily weighted than quality in the final grade.

Consider creating a safe environment to be a risk-management strategy as well. When people are in the process of learning, the number of mistakes increases as people fit the new ideas in with what they already know.

Second, the classroom must be oriented toward success. Think about creating an environment where you work toward more success rather than toward fewer failures.

There are four factors for success: the task itself; your genetic ability; luck; and your time, effort, and resources. The first three factors are generally out of a student's control. Therefore, when students choose to give of their time, effort, and resources, there must be some sort of positive payoff. It can be as simple as internal satisfaction over a job well done. Explicit expectations for any given task make it easier to focus on the appropriate outcome (rather than guessing and feeling unnecessarily disappointed).

Third, learning must be curiosity-driven. A community forms more easily when the classroom emphasis is on learning rather than memorization and grounded in creativity. In this environment, learners and teachers are constantly asking such questions as, "How else?" "I wonder?" "What about this way?" "In what ways might we. . . ?"" Curiosity is the main thing that keeps kids and teens engaged.

This inquiry-based structure teaches students that there are many paths and many answers to the questions at hand. Rather than competing to get the right answer, they benefit from working with others who have different viewpoints. The more ideas they have access to, the more creative a solution they stand to find.

Try setting up class-wide learning problems in which each person in the room has one necessary piece of information. The task could be a puzzle that requires math or logic to solve, once the pieces are assembled. For younger children, each student could have a clue that, assembled, allows them to guess a mystery item that will be important in the unit you are about to begin.

Fourth, in order to create a learning community, the group must be relationship-oriented. In order for real relationships to be possible, everyone must be known as an individual, and people must be allowed to contribute their expertise to the community. Inquiry-based tasks create this environment naturally; students get to know each other by contributing their unique ideas. (And they learn that they have unique ideas!)

The role of a functioning community is support, and that support can be

- Intellectual[5]—by contributing knowledge and talking through ideas.
- Emotional—by offering encouragement, recognition, and appreciation.
- Social—by acknowledging each member as a valued part of the group.
- Physical—by contributing skills and energy to complete the task.
- Moral—by encouraging others to do the right thing, even when no one else is present.

A classroom in which these forms of support are regularly present will have a lasting, positive effect on everyone involved.

As a result of such support, success is as much about relationships as it is about completing the task at hand. Every individual feels accountable to himself or herself as well as to the group. Even if the project fails, so long as everyone believes that every member did his or her best, the group remains intact.

Finally, in order to create a learning community, you as a teacher must ensure that choice is evident. Students must know that they have choices—to be involved, to use their unique abilities. Different students make different choices, and making that range evident in the classroom allows everyone to acknowledge different abilities.

Help students make the mental shift to working from areas of strength rather than from areas of weakness. For example, a student who focuses on weakness might think, "I am terrible at math; I am doing math problems so I will be less terrible." Seen positively, that student might say, "I am very organized. I recognize how I can use math to organize the world even better." Working in a group, students can choose the tasks that play to their strengths and rely on the contributions of others to achieve their shared goal. There is room for multiple intelligences and learning styles. As students feel more positive about their abilities, they begin to recognize how they can enrich the community.

If you find your students stuck in a rut of always working with the same people in small groups, you have several options. Telling students to work with someone new works some of the time, depending on how outgoing your students are. You could assign groups yourself. If student behavior allows, consider requiring students to sit in different seats when they walk into the room. Declare "Mix-it-up Monday" each week. (This is most easily implemented from the start of the year.) That way, when students turn to the person next door, that person changes weekly.

In order to get different students talking, consider assigning roles based on random (or not-so-random) characteristics. Announce that the person who reports to the class must be the person whose birthday is closest, who was sick most recently, who is wearing the brightest colors, and so on. The more students get accustomed to switching roles and working with new people, the more comfortable they will be.

In a traditional classroom, the end products (projects, lab experiments, papers, and so on) are for in-class eyes only. Their value is to demonstrate learning so that the teacher can give a grade. Students still learn content in a learning community, but with an added bonus: you are teaching them how to treat each other and how to work together to achieve a common goal. And if the end product can get displayed around the school, entered in a contest, or tied into a community event, so much the better.

Learning communities flatten the power structure in the classroom. Once you have laid the foundations for community and made its value explicit to your class, the rest is in the hands of your students. There are, after all, fifteen to thirty-five (or more) of them and only one of you. You empower students (and decrease the pressure on yourself) when you no longer have to be the sole source of knowledge and feedback.

The contributions of each of the students allow you as a teacher to make yourself dispensable. After all, you won't be around for them in the same way when the course is over.

By making the shift from a traditional classroom to a learning community, you are setting in motion a positive spiral of learning that will continue beyond the end of your class. You are empowering learners to continue acting in community-oriented ways when they become adults. Students learn that the whole is greater than the sum of its parts. They see that we are better when we work together—what a fantastic lesson for future citizens.

NOTES

1. Tuckman, Bruce W. "Developmental Sequence in Small Groups." *Psychological Bulletin* 65, no. 6 (1965): 384–99.

2. Egolf, Donald B. *Forming Storming Norming Performing*. Lincoln, NE.: Writers Club Press, 2001.

3. Lenciani, Patrick.. *The Five Dysfunctions of a Team* San Francisco, CA: Jossey-Bass, 2002.

4. Senge Peter. *The Fifth Discipline: The Art and Practice of the Learning Organization.* New York: Currency Doubleday, 1990, 219–20.

5. Lencioni, P. *The Five Dysfunctions of a Team.* San Francisco, CA: Jossey-Bass, 2002.

Chapter Nineteen

It's All Connected

We live in a cause-and-effect society. If you're reading this book during an election cycle, you need look no further than a political debate to hear how Leader X's policies directly caused a whole list of problems, which can only be solved by electing Candidate Y. If the economy is going down the toilet, if the schools are failing to meet standards, if global warming threatens our future, it's the fault of our current legislators (whichever party they happen to be from). It's the fault of big business, of bad morals, of the greed of the rich or the choices of the poor, and so on.

Regardless of the problem, you don't have to go far before you find people pointing toward the one single cause that they believe led to the whole thing. And if that one thing could just get fixed, all would be well.

Really?

Nothing is that simple.

The reality is that everything is interconnected. We are all part of the problem as well as part of the solution. Looking only for linear relationships, where x causes y, will only get us so far; as in learning, most relationships are circular. Frequently the problems that we face today are the results of yesterday's solutions. Those who look for fault rather than seeking new solutions tend to end up angry and stuck, without any new ideas for addressing issues at the generative level.

Of course, seeking dynamical understanding takes far more work than looking for someone or something to blame. It takes time, effort, and resources to understand the connections between the disparate problems around us. It takes work to comprehend the context. It also takes time, effort, and resources to consider how you are contributing to your problems and what you might have to do to be part of the solution.

Yet if we do not find those generative solutions, we end up recreating what has already been. Those who do not do some reflective learning of history, well, they're doomed to see the same problems repeated.

Given these complex challenges, the best work we can do is to look at our class as a system and see where there is leverage for change. The idea of leverage asks you to consider where to apply your time, effort, and resources so that things will actually change for the better and for the long run. Very frequently these leverage ideas are not about total reconstruction at one time. They are small beginning points—the first dominoes in the chain—so that cumulatively, we change in ways that are enduring and powerful.

Throughout this book, we've explored some of the key concepts of this complicated, fascinating world of teaching and learning. The ideas in any of these chapters might be a leverage point for your approach to the classroom. The leverage begins as soon as you start acting on one of them:

1. Reflect often and purposefully.
2. Everyone acts, thinks, and believes in ways that meet their needs.
3. You can't make anyone learn anything (unless they choose to).
4. Rules might regulate behavior, but values help us make the right choices in the long-term.
5. Perfect practice makes perfect.
6. Learning is a risky business. Make sure to work with safety nets.
7. First imagine, then decide . . . always in that order.
8. Know your audience!
9. What we laugh at, we tend to remember.
10. Be explicit! Communication is a two-way interaction.
11. Real and True makes learning relevant.
12. Your students (and you) are on a vision quest. Destination matters.
13. Find your own answers!
14. There are always multiple paths to the same place.
15. It's not what you understand, it's *how*.
16. Data tells a tale.
17. Partner with parents/guardians to help children succeed.
18. Create a space where everyone contributes.
19. You and your problems are part of the same system.

A good place to begin these leverage points is wherever you choose. Since they all involve you and you are part of the system, it really doesn't matter where you begin. They are all connected: as you begin to learn about one, other ideas begin to connect and become more powerful.

The joy of teaching is in the complexity. There is no one right way to run a classroom, no right or wrong entry point into understanding. Whatever in this book appeals to you at this point in time, knowing what you know (with your particular batch of students)—that's the perfect place to begin. A year from now, a completely different point might be appealing.

Peter Senge, in his writings about learning theory and organization, commented that there are two types of complexity: detail complexity and dynamic complexity. Detail complexity is what most of us would think of as complex. It describes a system with many different working parts and components.

Dynamic complexity is harder to comprehend. It describes a system with many loops and feedbacks. With dynamic complexity, the system of cause and effect is subtle—and not necessarily linear.

Our classrooms, like most of the complex systems of our day, have dynamic complexity. The effects of interventions over time are not always obvious. After all, the work you do in your classroom may make a difference in a student's learning three years down the road, and unfortunately, they don't always stop back in your class to tell you so.

The point of this chapter, then, is to invite you to begin to think more in terms of *influences* rather than causes. Thinking in terms of influences allows us to acknowledge the many different factors at work in our classrooms at any given time with a long-term view. There really are no quick fixes for complex systems.

Your students have years of prior experience that they bring with them that have profoundly influenced them. You have years of experience that have influenced who you are and how you do what you do every single day. And yet, new experiences can change you and your students. Like ripples in a pond, the influence of those leverage points can be far-reaching indeed.

When it comes to influencing students to learn and grow, time matters. It takes time to be willing to see things from new perspectives, time to learn new patterns of behavior, and time to deal with how you have changed. Explicitly addressing the time delay can lower frustration levels and accelerate your learning opportunities.

Every idea presented plays a role in how your classroom functions because, as we said at the start, you teach who you are. It is your classroom, your learning, your present, and your future—you decide what those changes are. Be confident in your decisions and flexible in your approach.

Have fun on your journey.

References

Ballard, Bruce. *The Curious Researcher*. New York: Pearson Longman, 2010.

Chabris, Christopher, and Daniel Simons. *The Invisible Gorilla*. Last modified June 19, 2011. http://www.theinvisiblegorilla.com.

Covey, Stephen R. *The 7 Habits of Highly Effective People: Powerful Lessons in Personal Change*. New York: Simon & Schuster, 1989.

Darling-Hammond, Linda. *The Flat World and Education: How America's Commitment to Equity Will Determine Our Future*. New York: Teachers College Press, 2010.

Dobbs, David. *National Geographic* (October 2011). http:ngm.nationalgeographic.com/2011/10/teenage-brains/dobbs-text

Egolf, Donald B. *Forming Storming Norming Performing: Successful Communications in Groups and Teams*. Lincoln, NE: Writers Club Press, 2001.

Hammerness, Karen, Linda Darling-Hammond, and John Bransford, with P. Grossman, F. Rust, and L. Shulman. "How Teachers Learn and Develop." In *Preparing Teachers for a Changing World: What Teachers Should Learn and Be Able to Do*, edited by Linda Darling-Hammond, John Bransford, Karen Hammerness, and Helen Duffy. San Francisco: Jossey-Bass, 2005: 358–389.

Kohn, Alfie. *Punished by Rewards: The Trouble with Gold Stars, Incentive Plans, A's, Praise, and Other Bribes*. New York: Mariner Books, 1999.

Kolis, M. *Student Relevance Matters*. Lanham, MD: Rowman & Littlefield, 2011.

Lencioni, P. *The Five Dysfunctions of a Team*. San Francisco, CA: Jossey-Bass, 2002.

Lenciani, Patricks. *Punished by Rewards: The Trouble with Gold Stars, Incentive Plans, A's, Praise, and Other BribesThe Five Dysfunctions of a Team*. San Francisco, CA: Jossey-Bass, 2002.

Marsh, Herbert W. "Do University Teachers Become More Effective with Experience? A Multilevel Growth Model of Students' Evaluations of Teaching over 13 Years." *Journal of Educational Psychology* 99, no.4 (2007): 775–790.

Mowrer, R. R., S. S. Love, and D. B. Orem. "Desirable Teaching Qualities Transcend the Nature of the Student." *Teaching of Psychology* 31, no. 2 (2004).

Palmer, Parker J. *The Courage to Teach: Exploring the Inner Landscape of a Teacher's Life*. Hoboken, NJ: John Wiley & Sons, 1998.

Peck, M. S. *The Different Drum: Community Making and Peace*. New York: Touchstone, 1998.

Senge, Peter M. *The Fifth Discipline: The Art & Practice of Learning Organization*. New York: Currency Doubleday, 2006.

Schmuck, R. A. and Schmuck, P. *Group Processes in the Classroom*, 8th ed. New York: McGraw-Hill, 2000.

Schön, Donald A. *The Reflective Practitioner: How Professionals Think in Action.* New York: Basic Books, 1983.

Tuckman, Bruce W. "Developmental Sequence in Small Groups." *Psychological Bulletin* 65, no. 6 (1965): 384–99.